Patrick —

Stepping Up

TO THE PLATE

Keep Stepping UP
to the Plate!

Donald L. ___

TO THE PLATE

INSPIRING INTERVIEWS
WITH MAJOR LEAGUERS

by David Kloser

Love
Your
Life

For information, write Love Your Life Publishing, P. O. Box 661274, Los Angeles, CA 90066

ISBN 0-9664806-2-7

Cover design by Michael Bernier
Interior design by Reider Publishing

Attention: Schools and Businesses

Love Your Life books are available at quantity discounts with bulk purchase for education, business, or sales promotional use. For information, please contact:

Special Sales Department, Love Your Life Publishing, P.O. Box 661274, Los Angeles, CA 90066.
www.LoveYourLife.com

Contents

Contents

To anyone who has had the courage to step up to the plate and go for their dreams.

Acknowledgments

A book like this could not be done alone. I had a team helping me, whether they knew it or not. So, I want to acknowledge all those people who supported, encouraged and allowed me the space to make my dreams come true.

Thank you to all the Major League teams for allowing me access to your clubhouses and players, specifically: Jay Alves, Jim Anderson, Brian Bartow, John Blake, Rob Butcher, Richard Cerrone, Steve Copses, Monique Giroux, Jon Greenberg, Sean Harlin, Tim Hevly, Jay Horwitz, Kerri Moore, Jim Moorehead, Lisa Ramsperger, Scott Reifert, Blake Rhodes, Rich Rice, Glen Serra, Kevin Shea, Chris Stathos, Jay Stenhouse, Bill Stetka, Bart Swain, Mike Swanson, Leigh Tobin, Jim Trdinich, Rick Vaughn, and Jim Young.

A very special thanks to John Olguin, Josh Rawitch, and Rachelle Smith of the Dodgers; Tim Mead and

Acknowledgments

Nancy Mazmanian of the Angels; Luis Garcia of the Padres; and Linda McNabb of the Miracle. You were all tremendous.

Thank you also to the hundreds of Major League players I interviewed, without you this book would only be a dream. Your graciousness with your time, energy and insights are greatly appreciated.

My sincere gratitude to Mike Veeck, without his help none of this would have happened.

Thank you to all my friends, teammates, and kids I coach for your valuable feedback on this project.

To my "All-star" team: Michael Bernier, Andrea Reider, Colleen Wilson, and Larry Donlin who went the extra innings to help with the production of this book.

To my "Home" team: my dad for signing me up for Little League, my mom for sewing all those patches on my first uniform, my sister Marybeth for her interest and support, my brothers Tim for always cheering me on and Trip for making the first call to get the ball rolling on this book. Thanks also to my nephews Matt, Greg, Riley and Brayden for reminding me to play.

To my loving wife and "MVP", Christine, for her acceptance, encouragement and support of me and my vision. I am the luckiest man on the face of the earth!

Introduction

Congratulations for stepping up to the plate. You now have in your hands some of the BEST collective wisdom gathered from Major League Baseball's top players. After you read this book, you'll see how the game of baseball relates to life in a whole new way.

During the 2003 and part of 2004 baseball season, I interviewed over 300 players to find out how the game of baseball taught them about life—both on and off the field. They made a point of sharing their personal stories and insights about the importance of teamwork, the meaning of success, how to overcome challenges and more. As a result, you've got an opportunity to learn from their experiences to become a better all-round person as well as improve as a player!

Like most kids, my first introduction to baseball was Little League, and my playing career went as far as college. I learned a lot of lessons from organized base-ball as well as pick-up games my buddies and I played in back yards, open streets or neighborhood fields. Other than my parents and family, baseball has been one of the major influences in my life and still is today.

Baseball's allowed me to feel sad, mad, nervous, and silly with joy. It's taught me the meaning of team-work, trust, discipline and perseverance. It's given me the opportunity to gain confidence, overcome failure and be humbled.

The experiences I've learned on the field have helped me get a better handle on the experiences I face off the field. Whenever I am challenged or need to understand something I ask myself, "How is what I'm going through now similar to something I've dealt with in baseball?" Once I figure out what the similari-ties are, I then ask myself, "How did I, or how would I, handle that situation in baseball?" Once I come up with an answer, I apply the 'baseball' concept to help me work through my current situation. I figure if I've experienced some sort of success or learned a lesson on the baseball field, it'll give me the confidence in life to face challenges at school, at home, with friends—pretty much anything.

Here's an example of what I mean. When I was in school, math was VERY hard. I remember a test I got back in which I didn't do very well. I was real mad because I missed questions I'd normally get right. Obviously, I wanted to do better. So I asked myself, "How is doing poorly on this math test similar to a situation in baseball?" ERRORS! Sometimes in games, I'd make an error on a play I'd normally make. The next day at practice, I'd work on fixing the error. I'd try to simplify things. For example, I'd ask someone to roll ground balls that I could easily field with my bare hands. Once I felt confident, I'd challenge myself a little more. I'd put my glove on and have someone hit me some light grounders. As my confidence grew, I'd field a lot of ground balls that were similar to the error I made in the game. After repeated success, I was no longer concerned about the error and felt completely confident to move on.

What's the baseball-life similarity in this example? There could be many, but for me it's going back to the basics and simplifying things. With my math test, I went back to easier problems to solve (just like fielding rolled grounders bare handed). Once I got the hang of that, I moved on to more challenging math problems to solve (like fielding ground balls with my glove). That helped to build my confidence and work on the types of problems I missed on the test (or baseball game).

Paul Molitor, Hall of Famer ('03), said, "Look at each day as a new opportunity." You have a new chance on the next play, the next test, or the next day. Learn from the past to make yourself better.

This book is more than just advice from Major League players on how to play baseball. It's a way for you to look for, and make the most of, opportunities by matching "life" situations with "baseball" situations.

That way you can have a better understanding and feel more confident in the things you do.

Lastly, whenever you feel you are up against a challenge, let this book be a source of inspiration. Allow it to help you take the proper actions and make the right choices, so you can reach out and help others just like these ball players have done for you.

Remember, these Major Leaguers were kids, just like you. They wanted to be heard, just like you. They had dreams, just like you. And they made their dreams come true, just like you can.

It's time to step up to the plate and play ball!

Editor's note: Players are listed by position played, team for whom they played when I interviewed them during 2003 and part of 2004, where they were born and awards they may have won throughout their career. Additionally, I recognize that English may not be the native language of some players. So in order to make the quotes more reader-friendly, slight modifications were made to keep the overall intention and meaning.

"I believe every individual is born with a talent.
The secret in life is to find out what that is,
and once you find it,
give it one hundred percent."
—BERNIE WILLIAMS

C H A P T E R 1

Why They Really Play the Game

*"There's nothing wrong with pursuing
your dreams and goals"*

—DAN PLESAC

I s it because they're good at it? Is it for the money?
Is it to be famous? Or could it be because they just
love what they do?

Why does anyone *really* do what they do? Perhaps
you've asked yourself similar questions like why
teachers teach, why astronauts shoot for the stars, or

why some people want to be doctors. What motivates someone to fly out of bed in the morning to start the day? Is it to follow a life-long dream?

What's your dream? What are some things that excite you? Is there a subject in school you like best? (other than recess!) What sparks your interest outside of school? Not every single player I talked with was born with a baseball glove and ball in their hand. Things change and people's interests change, too. You never know when you'll find something you love and become passionate about it.

I imagine people who wanted to become teachers, astronauts, doctors or whatever, made plenty of mistakes when they first started, but they stuck with it and learned a lot of lessons along the way. This is the case with just about everyone. Even Major League players didn't start out at the top of their game. So why did they keep playing? I asked them this very question. Most answers were as different as they are players, but interestingly enough, they fell into the categories of: Passion, Taking on Challenges, and Appreciation.

As you read through this chapter, you'll discover why these Major Leaguers chose the path of baseball. Maybe their stories will inspire you with your dreams.

Why do you play? What is your big dream?

PASSION

"My dad was a big baseball fan. As a young boy, you kind of look to your dad, so I took hold to it. When I take hold to something, I gain a passion for it. I started developing who my favorite players were. I started studying them. I tried to copy how they did things, everything from hitting, catching, and throwing. Everything they did, I would try to copy. I would just completely focus on that until I thought I had it. That's how I learned baseball."

Damion Easley, *infielder, Detroit Tigers.*
New York, New York. All-star.

"Ever since I was a kid, I had a ball and bat in my hand. There's nothing about baseball I don't like. I love practicing. I love spring training. I love the games. I love being in the clubhouse around all my friends. What's not to like about baseball?"

Steve Finley, *outfielder, Arizona*
Diamondbacks. Paducah, Kentucky.
4-time Gold Glove Winner. 2-time All-star.

"I love the competition. I love the game. I have a passion for the game. Every time I step on the field, that's where I am most comfortable. I don't have to be different. I don't have to make up stuff."

Eric Gagne, *pitcher, Los Angeles Dodgers.*
Montreal, Petit-Quebec, Canada. Cy Young
Award Winner, 2003. Rolaids Relief Winner,
2003. 2-time All-star.

TAKING STEPS

"I really had to pass a lot of tests to get to the Big Leagues . . ."
—ANDRES GALARRAGA

"I always loved this game. When I was a kid, I dreamed of being a professional baseball player. I thank God, who helped me with my dream to come true. It's not that easy as people think. It comes from a lot of work. I really had to pass a lot of tests to get to the Big Leagues and to stay in the Big Leagues for a long time. That is something you have to take in your heart, inside, to get better and better."

Andres Galarraga, *infielder, San Francisco Giants. Caracas, Venezuela. 2-time Gold Glove Winner. 5-time All-star.*

"I grew up in baseball because my father played in the Big Leagues for 12 years (Fred Kendall, ML career, 1969–1980). I think whenever I was old enough to have a ball in my hand, I did. That's all I ever wanted to do. I played every other sport, but baseball's in my blood."

Jason Kendall, *catcher, Pittsburgh Pirates. San Diego, California. 3-time All-star.*

"Since I was a four or five year-old, I dreamed of playing in the Big Leagues. That's why I think the game of baseball is so wonderful. It sets goals and makes you aim higher to what you want to achieve in life. Not just in baseball, but in life in general. I think baseball sets those goals and sets those priorities. Without hard work and determination you aren't going to be able to achieve those goals."

Joe McEwing, *utility player, New York Mets. Bristol, Pennsylvania.*

"Nothing happens until I throw a pitch. I'm in control of the tempo of the game and the speed of the game. That's just what I love. It's so much fun doing what I do. I get to play a kid's game for a living. What could be better than that?"

Mark Mulder, *pitcher, Oakland Athletics. South Holland, Illinois. All-star*

"It's something that, I think, every kid dreams about doing. To be able to live out a lifelong dream is something that not a lot of people can do. I look back at my career and I can remember spending many days in grade school, junior high and high school, dreaming about playing in the Big Leagues—playing for the Chicago White Sox, who were my favorite team. The thing I've gotten the most is, you realize there's nothing wrong with dreaming. There's nothing wrong with pursuing your dreams and goals. But the thing you have to do is, you have to be willing to pay the price to achieve those goals."

Dan Plesac, *pitcher, Philadelphia Phillies. Gary, Indiana. 3-time All-star.*

"I was kind of raised on playing baseball. My uncle Doc (Dwight) Gooden (ML career, 1984–2000) kind of made me interested in playing. He motivated and pushed me in that area because I was more of a football player. You have to have a love for anything you do. I don't care how much it pays you, you have to have pride in doing it."

Gary Sheffield, *outfielder, Atlanta Braves. Tampa, Florida. World Series Champion, 1997. 7-time All-star.*

"When you love the game, you're going to have more compassion and more of a desire to work hard. I just love the fact that you need nine guys going in the same direction at all times. There are a lot of different strategies involved with the lineup, pitch execution, and how to pitch to different hitters. I just had a love for the game because of my father when he played (Chris Speier, ML career 1971–1989). I initiated that love just from watching him play and going to the ballpark with him.

Justin Speier, *pitcher, Colorado Rockies. Walnut Creek, California.*

TAKING STEPS

*"You have to have a love
for anything you do."*

– GARY SHEFFIELD

"It's just being out there on the field and the camaraderie you have with your teammates. Not everyone has the passion for the game, but guys that continue with baseball, they have that passion. It's hard to describe, but once you have it, you know you have it."

Chase Utley, *infielder, Philadelphia Phillies. Pasadena, California.*

CHALLENGES

"It's the competition, even though it's a team sport. It's an individual competition, because it's the pitcher against the batter. You can only control so much and you got to rely on the rest of your teammates to help you out. Growing up as a kid, my mom put me in there to stay away from drugs and gangs and things like that. And once I played it, I fell in love with it."

Juan Acevedo, *pitcher, Toronto Blue Jays. Juarez, Mexico.*

"I loved being out there trying to figure out the situations. There are so many different things that can happen in the game of baseball that can affect the outcome. Baseball is truly a game of inches and situations. You have to always be prepared."

Mike Bordick, *infielder, Toronto Blue Jays.*
Marquette, Michigan. All-star.

"I just love the repetition, the constant work towards perfection with the swing and hitting. It's great because it's a team sport you play at an individual level. It's like an onion, there are so many different layers to the game."

Shawn Green, *outfielder, Los Angeles*
Dodgers. Des Plaines, Illinois. Gold Glove
Winner. 2-time All-star.

"I think there's no point in a baseball game where there is lost hope. There are a lot of sports where you're kind of stuck to a time limit. In baseball, the game is not over until the team gets the last out. At no point, I don't think, a team can give up or lose hope. You have to get the last out to finish the game."

Roy Halladay, *pitcher, Toronto Blue Jays.*
Denver, Colorado. Cy Young Award Winner,
2003. 2-time All-star

"In the United States, everybody plays basketball and football. In Japan we just play baseball. We don't play the other stuff. That's why, from when I was around 12 or 13 years old, I'm always playing in baseball. I'm a pitcher so we go more against the hitters, like a match up. That is a good part about baseball. Like basketball, you face five on five. But we've got a one to one. It's a team sport, but still it's face to face, one guy against one guy."

Shigetoshi Hasagawa, *pitcher,*
Seattle Mariners. Kobe, Japan. All-star.

"It's fun because it's hard. It's not an easy game. You get a lot of satisfaction out of doing well at it. Just like everything else in life, anything that's worth doing, is usually not easy to do. The harder you work, that's what makes it what it is. It's the work you put into it."

Paul Konerko, *infielder, Chicago White Sox.*
Providence, Rhode Island. All-star.

TAKING STEPS

"It's fun because it's hard."

—PAUL KONERKO

"I played basketball, baseball and football in high school. Baseball is just a challenge. It's you against the pitcher, you against the game, every day. You're going to have your good days and bad days. It teaches you a lot about dealing with life. Not every day is going to be the greatest day. Some days you're going to be faced with adversity. It just makes you stronger as a person."

Matt Lawton, *outfielder, Cleveland Indians. Gulfport, Mississippi. All-star.*

"You're constantly learning what your weaknesses are and what your strengths are. It's a game of adjustments. It seems like just when you make an adjustment, you figure something out, pitchers and teams make adjustments against you. Then you have to go back to the drawing board. Life is that way. You have to make adjustments. You have to learn how to deal with adversity and failure. More times than not, when you figure out what your strengths and weaknesses are, it makes you successful a little bit faster. The quicker you make those adjustments, the faster you are going to be successful. It is really similar to life."

Gary Matthews Jr., *outfielder, Baltimore Orioles. San Francisco, California.*

"I like baseball because you never know what is going to happen each and every day. It's very unpredictable. There has never been a team to win all 162 games and there never will be. Each day you come to the ballpark, you don't know what to expect. But you work off of basic fundamentals. Practice is very important with this game and repetition as well as discipline—a mental and a physical discipline. If you look at life, all of those things are very important as well."

Jamie Moyer, *pitcher, Seattle Mariners.*
Sellersville, Pennsylvania. All-star.

"The biggest thing is the competition. Growing up, the competition got better and better each level you went up. I know it's like that with any sport, but my sport was baseball. The real challenge I've always enjoyed facing, was to see if I can get better along with the other players—to see if I can challenge myself to be able to play with older kids, or kids that were more talented than I was at that age. That pushed me a little bit. It was exciting to find out that I could improve— I could get better. Even today, the point is to see how good you can get. You're competing against the best players pretty much in the world, and they're getting better too. When you're in the Minor Leagues and you get up to the Major Leagues and play against certain guys you watched on TV and you're actually facing them now, there's always a little question mark. You're wondering if you can really compete. It's fun being able to know that you can compete and do everything you can to try and improve."

Russ Ortiz, *pitcher, Atlanta Braves.*
Encino, California. All-star.

TAKING STEPS

*"Dealing with failure and turning
it into a positive experience
makes you a stronger person. . ."*
—JUNIOR SPIVEY

"One of the things that makes baseball so intriguing to me is the fact that there are so many games inside the game. There's the game between the pitcher and the hitter. All these different thought processes are going through nine different players' heads. There are just little games within the game that go on to make the big game pretty special."

Desi Relaford, *infielder, Kansas City Royals. Valdosta, Georgia.*

"It's a challenge. It's a great game because it's unpredictable. You don't know what's going to happen. It's a game of probabilities and percentages. If you go 3 out of 10, you're successful. It's a game of failure. Dealing with failure and turning it into a positive experience makes you a stronger person inside and out.

Junior Spivey, *infielder, Arizona Diamondbacks. Oklahoma City, Oklahoma. All-star.*

APPRECIATION

"I just always had a love for baseball because I was into the history of it. My father was always a St. Louis Cardinal fan. I lean more towards baseball that way because he and I would always go outside and play catch. It was always a bonding with my father."

Brian Boehringer, *pitcher, Pittsburgh Pirates. St. Louis, Missouri. World Series Champion, 1996.*

"Baseball was something that I was good at. It always seemed like I was picking something up and throwing it. I was always throwing a ball, a pinecone, dirt clod or whatever. I guess it kind of fit right in with what I always seemed to be doing, either with somebody or by myself. Maybe that had a large influence."

Kevin Brown, *pitcher, Los Angeles Dodgers. Milledgeville, Georgia. World Series Champion, 1997. 6-time All-star.*

"It's a very unique game, in the sense that you physically score the run rather than the ball. There are so many dimensions to the game. It's more strategic. It has an element that's one on one, but at the same time it's a team game. My older brother taught me about the game and I learned from an early age to really love it."

Doug Glanville, *outfielder, Texas Rangers. Hackensack, New Jersey.*

"You learn how to appreciate the skills that each player has and their assets to the game. There are guys who are good pinch hitters. There are guys who are power hitters. There are leadoff hitters. There are base stealers. There are so many different types of players that you need on the team to be successful."

Luis Gonzalez, *outfielder, Arizona Diamondbacks. Tampa, Florida. World Series Champion, 2001. 4-time All-star.*

"I had baseball in my family. My dad played some ball. I had four uncles on my mom's side that were all catchers. So I was the pickle guy in the front yard. We would be out there for hours. I always had a glove around. I was always outside banging the ball off of grandma's awning in the front yard or hitting them in the street chasing them all the way down the block. It's funny, the older I got it, even up to high school, I was just playing because it was a blast. I was out there with my friends. I really didn't think about the other team. I just thought about hitting the ball, catching the ball and throwing the ball—keeping it simple, like you were a Little Leaguer. The basics of the game are the same. That's what we're always striving to get back to is seeing the ball as long as you can, hitting the ball as hard as a can; catching and throwing the ball, running and getting dirty. We always try to revert back to being a kid. I think that would parallel life, because we have to be kid-minded a lot of times in life. I learned that from my hitting coach, Rick Downing. He was with the Dodgers when I was with the Dodgers. He had this one little saying, "Just remember K.I.S.S. Keep It Simple Stupid". And I will never forget it."

Dave Hansen, *infielder, San Diego Padres. Long Beach, California.*

"I grew up playing tennis, which is an individual sport and golf, things like that. When baseball came around, I finally learned about teamwork and camaraderie and pulling for each other, pulling for your friends and teammates."

Bo Hart, *infielder, St. Louis Cardinals. Creswell, Oregon.*

"All my family plays. My dad, my brothers and all my cousins—everybody play baseball. When I was young, I wanted to continue to follow my dad and my brothers. When I lived in Cuba, it's the number one sport. So I started to play on the team when I was nine years old because I couldn't start any earlier. When I started to play baseball, this is the sport I liked and the sport I wanted to be good at."

Livan Hernandez, *pitcher, Montreal Expos. Villa Clara, Cuba. World Series Champion, 1997. World Series MVP, 1997.*

"Like a lot of kids who enjoy sports, I played on a year-round basis. There was just something, especially coming out of a cold climate, when the spring would come around and the snow would melt. You get your dad to take you out in the backyard and play catch and wait for the season to start whether it's T-ball or Little League. A lot of ways baseball is a sport of renewal. I was growing up in Minnesota and having a chance to follow professional baseball was something I became attached to, whether it was listening to the radio in my bed at night or envisioning things happening that I was hearing being described by a play-by-play guy on the radio. There was something about it that caught my fancy more than the other sports. I didn't really decide—it just kind of happened that that's where my passion fell."

Paul Molitor, *Hall of Fame 2003, infielder (ML career, 1978-1998), Milwaukee Brewers, Toronto Blue Jays, Minnesota Twins. St. Paul, Minnesota. World Series Champion, 1993. World Series MVP, 1993. 7-time All-star.*

TAKING STEPS

"There's nothing more special than knowing that your mother and father are very proud of what you're doing."

—JOSE VIDRO

"Baseball was the first sport I played when I was ten in Korea. When I started baseball basically, it was the only sport I played until now. That's how I grew up in my culture. Only one sport you can play in school, junior high school and high school. Here, the kids play football, basketball and other sports at the same time. But in Korea I can't do that, so I play one. Baseball is obviously my life. I made a dream when I was young to be the best baseball player and make professional. So I work hard and practice a lot. And now I made it as a professional player and now my dreams came true. I have other opportunities for my country as a Korean. I have two things to do, trying to be a good baseball player and trying to be an idol for kids over here and especially in Korea, my home country."

Chan Ho Park, *pitcher, Texas Rangers.*
Kongju, South Korea. All-star.

"Ever since I was about four or five years old, I always wanted to be a Major League Baseball player. As I look back on my childhood, it was something that my dad and I got to share as a life experience growing up. Whether it was taking ground balls in the backyard, or my dad throwing batting practice to me at the Little League park or going to the batting cages, I have a lot of memories that are tied to baseball. My dad was my coach for the majority of my youth. I got a chance to play on the same team as my little brother Richard. Those are things that stand out in my childhood."

Mike Sweeney, *infielder, Kansas City Royals.*
Orange, California. 4-time All-star.

"In my country (Cuba), we do not have that many sports to choose. Baseball and boxing—that's the only sport they give you the opportunity for us to get out of the country and be somebody. Our country is not like here. You have basketball, hockey and football. We don't have too many of those things in my time. I love baseball because my father used to play baseball. My uncle used to play and that's all you grew up on. I think it's a great game. If I were born again, I would play baseball. But you need your education."

Luis Tiant, *pitcher (ML career, 1964-1982), Cleveland Indians, Minnesota Twins, Boston Red Sox, New York Yankees, Pittsburgh Pirates, California Angels. Marianao, Cuba. 3-time All-star.*

"What I love the most, is when I go back home and I see my son talking about baseball and how (my family) feels when they see me on TV playing games. That makes me feel and know that my family is proud of what I do. There's nothing more special than knowing that your mother and father are very proud of what you're doing."

Jose Vidro, *infielder, Montreal Expos. Mayaguez, Puerto Rico. 3-time All-star.*

Step up to the challenge:

- Which Major League player or players do you relate with most about why you do what you do?
- What are some other things that excite you the way baseball does? It could be a certain subject in school, or a hobby you like to do, or a place you like to visit.
- What are the things you like to do because of the challenge? Out of appreciation? Because of your passion about it?

 ## Step out of the box to look for the signs

Try this for a week: As you go about your day, start to notice why you "play the game" in the things you do. In other words, why do you *really* do the things you do? Is it out of passion, the challenge or from appreciation? Begin to notice why other people do what they do. You might even ask someone, "Why do you really do what you do?"

Who Wants To
Be On My team?

"Be a fountain, not a drain."

—TREVOR HOFFMAN

Who makes up a team?

Obviously players or teammates do. But MAK-ING the team is only half of it. What's important is WHAT you bring to the team and HOW you bring it. And I don't mean just bringing your glove and your bat. I'm talking about what you contribute to the team. Your contribution as a teammate has an effect on how much success you'll have personally as well as how much success the team will have.

I look at a teammate as being more than just a player on a baseball team (or any sports team). Let's take it a step further. A teammate is anyone with whom you participate or spend time. For example: your family is a team; your friends are a team, your classmates and the people you hang out with at school are another team. So, whether you know it or not, you "play" on many different teams throughout your day. Remember, it's what you bring to these teams and how you bring it.

Here's another example: say you're invited to your best friend's birthday party. The party is the team and the guests are teammates. The "what" that you bring to the party is your friendship and a gift for your best friend. The "how" is about caring and respect. Did you make an effort to show up on time to the party? Did you get something cool that your friend would like or could you've cared less about what you brought?

When I spoke with the Major Leaguers about teammates, I found there were basically two kinds—players they would *want* on their team and players they would definitely *not want* on their team.

The categories their comments fell into were: Effort, Support, and Respect. As you read through the chapter, see if you can tell which kind of teammate the players are talking about. Their answers may surprise you!

EFFORT

"You have to be disciplined in this game. You could have great talent, but if you have a bad attitude, it's not great for anybody. So my guy should be a guy with great talent, plays with heart and has great discipline of the game."

Edgardo Alfonzo, *infielder, San Francisco Giants. Santa Teresa, Venezuela. All-star.*

"I want a player on my team who goes out there and plays hard and plays the right way. He gives everything he has to the club in order to try and win a baseball game. I don't care what guys' reputations are. I mean I do care, but that's not something I have to have. I like to have guys that go out and play the game hard and play it right."

Jeff Bagwell, *infielder, Houston Astros. Boston Massachusetts. NL Rookie of the Year, 1991. NL MVP, 1994. Gold Glove Winner. 4-time All-star.*

"It's somebody who comes here for the paycheck. He hopes he doesn't get in the game because he doesn't want to screw up and he's afraid to play. And there are those people. You find out, at some point, what everybody on your team is like and everybody else realizes it too. More times than not, those teammates aren't teammates for very long. People get shuffled in and out constantly for a whole lot less then just not playing well. Sometimes you have a guy on a team that's maybe not the most talented, but shows up every day and busts his tail. Those are the people you want to surround yourself with as opposed to people who don't care, are in it for themselves, afraid to play or constantly say they can't play. And that's every day life too. There are people who do that everywhere. Those people don't usually hang around too long."

Rod Beck, *pitcher, San Diego Padres. Burbank, California. NL Rolaids Relief Winner. 3-time All-star.*

"They put the team first. They're responsible. They're conscientious. My mom and dad always told me to be responsible. It's like saying, 'Do the right thing'. The right thing isn't always the easy thing to do. It's not always the easiest path to take or the one that's going to make you the most popular. In the end, it's always the right way to go."

Craig Counsell, *infielder, Arizona Diamondbacks. South Bend, Indiana. World Series Champion, 1997.*

TAKING STEPS

"I want a player on my team who goes out there and plays hard and plays the right way."

—JEFF BAGWELL

"Somebody who's just negative all the time, whining, never has anything good to say. Selfish. You don't like to be around them because they can bring a whole team down."

Carl Crawford, *outfielder, Tampa Bay Devil Rays. Houston Texas.*

"A great teammate doesn't have to be a star on the team. A great teammate can be anyone from the number one guy to the 25th guy. It's the example he leads in the clubhouse and off the field. Some guys you look to as an example. Some guys you look to, to encourage you. If you get one guy that can do all those things, that's a wonderful teammate."

Joe Girardi, *catcher, St. Louis Cardinals. Peoria, Illinois. World Series Champion, 1996, 1998, 1999. All-star.*

"Selfish people who are just worried about themselves. They don't show up to play every day. They feel like they deserve some kind of special treatment. I just don't pay them any attention. I try to stay as far away from them as possible."

Todd Helton, *infielder, Colorado Rockies.* Knoxville, Tennessee. *2-time Gold Glove Winner. 4-time All-star.*

"Someone who is genuinely into the game. Whether he is playing nine innings or not playing at all, there's a way you can help the ball club. It's being supportive. Mark Langston (ML career, 1984–1999) always said, 'Be a fountain and not a drain'. Always find a way to build someone up instead of break them down."

> **Trevor Hoffman,** *pitcher, San Diego Padres.*
> *Bellflower, California. Rolaids Relief Award*
> *Winner. 4-time All-star.*

"My biggest thing is competitiveness; never giving up an at-bat, diving after balls you think you can catch, never being afraid to take the ball as a pitcher, and go out there and take your best against anybody. So many times you run into people that give in. When you can find a teammate that can go out there and give you 100% every day and then be there for every one of his teammates, that's big for me. Anybody in this clubhouse ever needs anything, there's a pretty good chance there's 25 guys who will be there to help him."

> **Troy Percival**, *pitcher, Anaheim Angels.*
> *Fontana, California. 4-time All-star.*
> *World Series Champion, 2002.*

"Someone you can count on. There's no guessing what you're going to get. Somebody who can be held accountable and you can trust that they're going to do what they're going to do, preparation-wise."

> **Tim Salmon,** *outfielder, Anaheim Angels.*
> *Long Beach, California. AL Rookie of the*
> *Year, 1993. World Series Champion, 2002.*

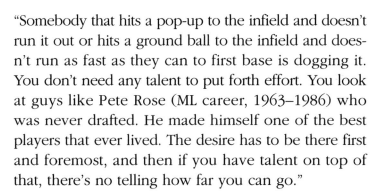

TAKING STEPS

"A great teammate doesn't have to be a star on the team."

—JOE GIRARDI

"Somebody that hits a pop-up to the infield and doesn't run it out or hits a ground ball to the infield and doesn't run as fast as they can to first base is dogging it. You don't need any talent to put forth effort. You look at guys like Pete Rose (ML career, 1963–1986) who was never drafted. He made himself one of the best players that ever lived. The desire has to be there first and foremost, and then if you have talent on top of that, there's no telling how far you can go."

> **Matt Williams**, *infielder, Arizona Diamondbacks. Bishop, California. 4-time Gold Glove Winner. 2-time All-star. World Series Champion, 2001.*

SUPPORT

"When I came up to the Big Leagues, a lot of veterans on the team helped me out. When I was doing things right, they'd comment on it. When I was doing things wrong, they'd comment on it also. I made mistakes less and less because I was warned about them. Now

I'm 100% more knowledgeable about the rights and wrongs of baseball, just the little things. I owe a lot to the veterans who took me aside and made me realize and understand the game that much more."

Sean Burroughs, *infielder, San Diego Padres. Atlanta, Georgia.*

"You surround yourself with positive people you feel you can talk to and they pump you up to build confidence. Baseball is built on confidence. The guy I want to be around is confident and positive. A guy that is negative is always talking about, 'He can't do this or they're trying to do this'. You always got guys with excuses, so I just try to stay away from guys that are lazy and don't care. In this game you have to care."

Torii Hunter, *outfielder, Minnesota Twins. Pine Bluff, Arkansas. 3-time Gold Glove Winner. All-Star.*

TAKING STEPS

"We help each other out and support each other like a friend."

—HIDEO NOMO

"A great teammate is a guy who's going to let you know, 'Hey you look like you're dragging a little bit', but between you and me quietly. He's a guy that's going to pat you on the back when you're doing well. When you're not doing well, still pat you on the back and say, 'I'm behind you'. That means a lot. Sometimes he doesn't have to say anything."

> **Charles Johnson,** *catcher, Colorado Rockies.*
> *Fort Pierce, Florida. 4-time Gold Glove*
> *Winner. World Series Champion, 1997.*
> *2-time All-Star.*

"I look at teammates as supporting each other or becoming competitive with each other to make each other better. Every day we go through a lot of different times together. We overcome those difficult times. We help each other out and support each other like a friend."

> **Hideo Nomo**, *pitcher, Los Angeles Dodgers.*
> *Osaka Japan. NL Rookie of the Year, 1995.*
> *All-star.*

"It's a game that demands enthusiasm and support. Encouragement goes a long way, whether you're somebody's teammate or coach. He or she is going to go through bad times just like you or I would. Just because somebody makes a mistake doesn't mean that you shouldn't be there to encourage them through it. I've often said that a pat on the back goes a long way. When somebody was there to pump me up and encourage me, it gave me the incentive to want to do better. To me, that makes the difference in a lot of guys' days or a lot of guys' seasons. I think that's very, very important."

> **Lance Parrish**, *coach, Detroit Tigers. Clairton, Pennsylvania. 3-time Gold Glove Winner. World Series Champion, 1984. 8-time All-star.*

"Somebody that's going to be supporting you all the time no matter if you're doing good or bad. There's a lot of jealousy in this game. Guys will be struggling and sometimes won't have anything to do with you if you're not going good. That's what I call the quality of a terrible teammate. You want to have somebody who has a good attitude. Someone who is humble and takes everything in stride."

> **Andy Pettitte**, *pitcher, New York Yankees. Baton Rouge, Louisiana. World Series Champion, 1996, 1998, 2000. 2-time All-star.*

"Somebody you can depend on, somebody who's going to be there through thick and thin. Just like anybody in your life. Coming to the Minor-League system and going away from home at 18, my teammates became my family. They're the people that I rely on day in and day out to be there for me emotionally and physically on and off the field. They take care of you and you take care of them."

Josh Phelps, *infielder, Toronto Blue Jays.*
Anchorage, Alaska.

"He puts the team before himself. I'm not a big fan of sarcastic people or negative people. I like being around guys who are always positive. Guys who can take the time to pat a teammate on the back. It's somebody going out of his way to lift somebody else even when they are struggling."

Gregg Zaun, *catcher, Colorado Rockies.*
Glendale, California.

"A teammate who doesn't want to play with everyone else. He wants to go out and do his own thing. He doesn't want to do something the way a coach tells him to do it when it might help him. He's not coachable."

Chad Zerbe, *pitcher, San Francisco Giants.*
Findlay, Ohio.

RESPECT

"A guy that's a team player is not afraid to share secrets, like Carlos Delgado. Every time we come to the ballpark he wants to go over the pitcher we're facing that night. He wants to tell me what he does at the plate against the pitcher. A (team player) cares about the team, cares about how each and every individual is doing. I've been around a lot of players like that, (such as) Alex Rodriguez and Carlos on this team."

Frank Catalanotto, *outfielder,*
Toronto Blue Jays. Smithtown, New York.

"Guys that try to be different. They don't always look out for other guys. They're just worried about what they do and how they fare on the field. They think the world revolves around them. First impressions mean a lot. I think a guy you don't want to play with is a guy who is selfish, arrogant."

Mike Fetters, *pitcher, Minnesota Twins.*
Van Nuys, California.

TAKING STEPS

"It's not your job to put that guy down because he's not doing it how you could do it . . ."
—JACQUE JONES

"Somebody that roots for everybody. Wants to win. He's going to do the little things, like good base running, great defense. Not always the best teammates are the best players. They're the ones with the best attitude that guys get along with and look up to. They play the game hard. Guys you can look to for answers, or can help you through the tough times because this game is tough and it wears on you."

Jason Giambi, *infielder, New York Yankees. West Covina, California. AL MVP, 2000. 4-time All-star.*

"I learn from everybody both good and bad qualities. That's how you learn. You take the bad from the bad qualities in people and you learn from that because you say, 'Hey, I'm not going to do that. That's not me'. You got a job to do each and every day here. Play the game. The quality of a good person stays focused and he knows what he's doing the next day. He knows what it's all about. He knows what life is all about. I just stay away from (the bad teammate). I go my different ways and he goes his different ways. That's how I handle things."

Eddie Guardado, *pitcher, Minnesota Twins. Stockton, California. 2-time All-star.*

"If you're putting down other players for making mistakes, I don't like that. When I was younger, I used to get mad and say things like, 'Man, he's messing up.' Then I'd step back and say, 'I don't make every single play. He's trying to do the best he can to make every play.' It's not your job to put that guy down because he's not doing it how you could do it or how you think he should be doing it. When you worry about yourself, and you make sure everything is right with you, and you're out there doing everything you can to help your team win, that's the guy I want to be with."

> **Jacque Jones**, *outfielder, Minnesota Twins. San Diego, California.*

"My ideal teammate is somebody that works hard to help the team. He respects the space of his teammates inside the clubhouse, on the plane, on the bus—the working environment, if you want to call it that. Somebody that takes pride in his performance, both on and off the field."

> **Greg Maddux,** *pitcher, Atlanta Braves. San Angelo, Texas. 4-time Cy Young Award Winner. 13-time Gold Glove Winner. World Series Champion, 1995. 8-time All-Star.*

"The ones who are constantly looking out for their own well-being, those are the ones who you find are not trusted. They aren't anybody that the other players confide in. The guys who you're with consistently for the month and a half of spring training or six months of the season, they really see what you are made of. They see whether your face is sincere and what your motivation is. They see what kind of person you truly are."

Mike Matheny, *catcher, St. Louis Cardinals.*
Columbus, Ohio. 2-time Gold Glove Winner.

"The best guys I've ever played with were like kids. They just let things slide off them. I played with George Brett (Hall of Fame, 1999. ML career, 1973–1993) He really didn't let things bother him. If he made an out, he'd go get 'em next time. He was really in the moment. The best guys I played with were in the moment. They really stay focused. Mike Sweeney is a great teammate. He's there for you when you make an out or do well. When he's at bat, he's focused. When he's rooting guys on, he's focused. He's just right there all the time."

Brent Mayne, *catcher, Kansas City Royals.*
Loma Linda, California.

"You win as a team and you lose as a team. I am around my teammates for about eight months out of the year. Whether you like them or dislike them, you have to find a way to get along. You learn about yourself and you learn about other people."

Jamie Moyer, *pitcher, Seattle Mariners. Sellersville, Pennsylvania. All-star.*

"Somebody that doesn't respect the game. I have played with some players that maybe have been good players, but not good teammates. It's guys, who come to the (ballpark) and don't feel like playing that day and kind of go through the motions. Those are the days you really figure out who the quality guys are on your team. For the most part, it's somebody that doesn't respect the game. You can't rely on them, day in and day out to give you a hundred percent."

Phil Nevin, *infielder, San Diego Padres. Fullerton, California. All-star.*

"Somebody who's a leader of the team can have a huge impact on the team. He might be the best player on the team, but it doesn't matter because he's making other players on the team feel bad by bringing them down (when they make) a bad play."

John Olerud, *infielder, Seattle Mariners. Seattle, Washington. 3-time Gold Glove Winner. World Series Champion, 1992, 1993. 2-time All-star.*

"I played with one of the best pitchers I ever caught in my life. He's out of baseball right now because of the way he acted. Nobody liked him because he was always talking bad about people. He didn't talk to the fans. And he is still a good pitcher."

Eddie Perez, *catcher, Milwaukee Brewers.*
Ciudad Ojeda, Venezuela.

"You always want to have good teammates to motivate yourself and to get yourself better. You want to be a winner and you need to look at what you can do to help your team to win. That's what it's all about, helping each other out like a brother. You spend more time in the season with your teammates then you spend with your family in the off-season."

Albert Pujols, *infielder, St. Louis Cardinals.*
Santo Domingo, Dominican Republic.
NL Rookie of the Year, 2001. 2-time All-star.

"Treat people with respect around you. Treat the game with respect. That's the ideal teammate. They are accountable. They say, 'Hey, I made an error today and it cost us the game. I take full responsibility for that. I make no excuses for my play or who I am.'"

Scott Rolen, *infielder, St. Louis Cardinals.*
Evansville, Indiana. NL Rookie of the Year,
1997. 5-time Gold Glove Winner. 2-time
All-star.

"The most important thing is that my teammates respect each other, like a family."

> **Alfonso Soriano**, *infielder, New York Yankees. San Pedro de Macoris, Dominican Republic. 2-time All-star.*

"A guy that leads by example, not so much a guy who tells you what to do or how things are done, but you watch the person and see how they go about their business. That's what I believe makes a good leader. I think it's also somebody who thinks of others before himself. If you're concerned more with people, you're not going to be focused on what's going on bad or if you're in a slump. If you help other people you're usually not going to focus so much on yourself."

> **Steve Sparks**, *pitcher, Detroit Tigers. Tulsa, Oklahoma.*

"The better you are as an individual, the more it helps the team. If you take care of what you know you are supposed to take care of, and do the things that are right, you will be better off with the people around you, whether it's your friends or your teammates."

> **Woody Williams**, *pitcher, St. Louis Cardinals. Houston, Texas. All-star.*

Step up to the challenge:

- If you were making up a "team", what qualities would you want in a teammate? How similar are they to the players you read about in this chapter?
- Using the example of a birthday party (from the chapter introduction) to figure out what a teammate brings, how well do you receive or get along with your teammates?
- What can you learn and appreciate about the qualities in your opponents—the "players" on other "teams" (or people with whom you don't hang out)?

 ## Step out of the box to look for the signs

Try this for a week: As you go about your day, start to notice how people on other "teams" act. What are the reasons you MIGHT want to be on their team? What are the reasons you wouldn't want to be on their team?

CHAPTER 3

I Don't Think I Smell, But They Tell Me I Stink!

"God, give me strength to get through this and not act in a way like he's acting."

—MIKE SWEENEY

"Booooo! You stink! You're a bum! Hey catcher, you can't throw anyone out. You probably couldn't throw out the garbage! You're the worst pitcher I've ever seen! You've got no business wearing that uniform. You can't hit. You're terrible!" And on and on it goes.

It happens from game to game, stadium to stadium, and city to city. When you go to a game and you hear the fans booing or calling players names, do you ever wonder what the player is thinking? Sure the players are tough, but do you think it hurts their feelings? How do they deal with all that heckling?

Baseball can be difficult to play even without fans and players screaming and yelling at you. We've all been yelled at, called names and teased for a variety of reasons—some more than others. And it can be challenging not to get wrapped up in what people are saying and yelling at you.

Some players believe if they hear something enough times, there must be some truth to it; so then they start to believe it. The key is to recognize the difference between someone's opinion about you as a player, and the truth. Catcher, Greg Zaun said, "I don't reflect upon myself as a poor player, just a player that had a poor performance." (More about that in chapter 4).

So, if we know teasing is going to happen and people are going to yell and scream at us and call us names, what can we do about it? How can we make the best of the situation? What do the pros do to stay positive in a game that is built on failure and can be negative? That's what this chapter is about—Big Leaguers really letting you know what they think about hecklers, but more importantly, how they handle being teased and called names.

"I don't want to say I don't care, because I do. You have to concentrate on what you're going to do. And I already have my mind set on what I'm going to listen to, what I have to do, or what my intentions are. Friends call me up and they say, 'Man, you look really mad, on TV'. I say, 'No, that's the way I play'. I like to concentrate as soon as I walk into the clubhouse and as soon as I walk out. It's only three or four hours. I don't want to take my focus off what I'm concentrating on."

Edgardo Alfonzo, *infielder, San Francisco Giants. Santa Teresa, Venezuela. All-star.*

"Don't pay any attention to it. That's easy to say. If you prioritize the people that you care about, then anyone else that doesn't know what they're talking about—it's not going matter what they think. If you care about what your coach, your teammates and your family think, it keeps it pretty simple. You're not going to worry about somebody that doesn't know or care about you."

David Bell, *infielder, Philadelphia Phillies. Cincinnati, Ohio.*

TAKING STEPS

"You go through (the bad stuff). It still hurts. You got to go on."
—BRET BOONE

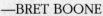

"It's experience. You go through the bad stuff. It still hurts. You got to go on. I remember I had a real tough year in 1997. I was getting booed by the end of the year and booed loud. You got to be a professional. (I remember) walking out to lunch with my wife and having people look at you thinking, 'What's wrong with you? You stink.' That's a bad feeling. On the other side, I've had unbelievable years where you walk down the street and people treat you like you're the king. There are pluses and there are minuses."

Bret Boone, *infielder, Seattle Mariners. El Cajon, California. 3-time Gold Glove Winner. 3-time All-star.*

"I just remain focused on what I'm trying to do. Maybe in my younger days I might react to it. Now, it means nothing. How did I get to that point? I realize what I'm trying to do. I'm trying to help the team by doing my job successfully. And the only way I can do my job is to be 100% focused on it. If I'm thinking about, 'this guy's a jerk' because he's yelling at me or saying I stink, that's a distraction. I just learned what I needed to focus on to do my job successfully and that was not part of it."

Jeromy Burnitz, *outfielder, Los Angeles Dodgers. Westminster, California. All-star.*

"There are times when people get on you, you're thinking, 'That's mean. Why would you say that to somebody just because we are baseball players?' We're still human beings. We don't go to somebody's office and sit over them and say, 'You're not typing right! That was a terrible phone call you just made! You stink. You're a bum!' That gets old after awhile. You treat people the way you want to be treated.

For example: A guy got on me the other night. He's yelling, 'Cut your hair! Cut your hair!' every time I came up to bat. I think he had a few drinks. I wanted to be mean back, but instead, I brought him a glass of water. I said, 'Here you go. You might want to have this so you feel better tomorrow morning'. He kind of lightened up and said, 'Thanks a lot for the water!' When people get on me, I kill them with kindness. I'm going to show you that I'm a nice guy and what you're saying to me is not affecting me.

When people yell at you, they want you to yell back. That's not the way to go. If you snap and play his game, now you're yelling at him and he's yelling at you. What does that accomplish? What does it accomplish when two people fight? It accomplishes nothing. If you can talk about it and get things out, I think that's a better way to go."

Sean Casey, *infielder, Cincinnati Reds.*
Willingboro, New Jersey. 2-time All-Star.

"Nobody likes to be called names. We are no different than a Little Leaguer. I don't really think it's your friends calling you names. It's people who don't know you. How would they know anything about me? That's how I look at it, actually. If people I really respect are calling me names, then you take that to heart a little more. People who don't know me, it kind of rolls off my back."

Craig Counsell, *infielder, Arizona Diamondbacks. South Bend, Indiana. World Series Champion, 1997.*

"People will call you names out of the blue ever since you were in Little League. To be honest, the only way you can get used to that is to continue to go through it. It's an ugly side of the game, but you know what? It's there. Either let it bother you, or you can let it make you stronger. You just have to accept that it's not personal and you can't take it with emotion."

Darin Erstad, *outfielder, Anaheim Angeles. Jamestown, North Dakota. 2-time Gold Glove Winner. World Series Champion, 2002. 2-time All-star.*

"You try to block everything out. When I was young I always got teased and all that stuff. People who talk bad are always jealous of you anyway. I think it's just a waste of time to worry about it. It's just a waste of energy. It's negative. You got to think positive and not worry about these guys. I don't."

> **Eric Gagne**, *pitcher, Los Angeles Dodgers, Montreal, Petit-Quebec, Canada. Cy Young Award Winner, 2003. Rolaids Relief Winner, 2003. 2-time All-star.*

"I just have fun with it. If they rag you, just say, "You're right." Fans want guys to bark back at them or curse back at them. Then they're going to rag you even more. But if you just smile and say, 'You're right', usually they don't have much left to say. That's all part of the fun."

> **Mark Grace**, *infielder, Arizona Diamondbacks. Winston-Salem, North Carolina. 4-time Gold Glove Winner. 3-time All-star. World Series Champion, 2001.*

TAKING STEPS

"Either let it (teasing) bother you, or you can let it make you stronger."

—DARIN ERSTAD

"I just let them have their fun. We're going to be playing this game for as long as we can. They get their one time to shine. They come to one game and they feel like it's their opportunity to rag us. We understand that. I guess you could say that's part of the game. Just as long as it doesn't get personal. When that happens, we find a security guard and tell them to get them out of there. And the security guards are great around the league, especially here. There is a zero tolerance here for that. They kick them out and the problem is solved. If you yell back at them or cuss back at them, that just makes you look bad for the (people) around that see that."

Danny Graves, *pitcher, Cincinnati Reds. Saigon, South Vietnam. All-star.*

"You have to realize in this game, people are going to try to take you out of your game. And the way to do that is by personal attacks or personal shots—calling you names and stuff like that. Part of being successful is learning how to tune all that stuff out and staying focused on what is happening between the lines. You're concentrating on that given pitcher and what you're going to do with the ball when and if it's hit to you. You focus in on the game and not what's going on outside the lines. Once you achieve that, then the sky's the limit for you."

Chipper Jones, *outfielder, Atlanta Braves. DeLand, Florida. NL MVP, 1999. World Series Champion, 1995. 5-time All-star.*

TAKING STEPS

"Part of being successful is learning how to tune all that stuff out."

—CHIPPER JONES

"What I found out was they wouldn't rag you if they didn't think you were good. But if you are good and they know you are good and they know that you have the ability to change the game in your team's favor, that's when they get on you. As crazy as it sounds, that's a sign of respect. When somebody is ragging and they're constantly on you, they have a lot of respect for you or else they wouldn't bother you."

Jacque Jones, *outfielder, Minnesota Twins. San Diego, California.*

"To me, I take it in stride. I was a short chubby kid when I was little. So I got a lot of razzing and stuff like that. I still get razzed here because I'm short. I just laugh. You have to take it right in stride. You can't take it serious because you're going to get ripped more often than not. Have fun with it. If you take it serious, it starts getting in your head. It doesn't bother me."

Paul Lo Duca, *catcher, Los Angeles Dodgers. Brooklyn, New York. All-star.*

"When those things happen and people call me names, I use it as a tool. Focus and concentration are very important to me. If I'm pitching and I hear somebody in the stands, or even in the upper deck, saying, 'Moyer you stink!' or 'throw strikes', that tells me that I'm not focused. I try not to let it draw my attention away. I say, 'This tells me I'm not focusing. I need to step off the rubber and try to refocus.'"

> **Jamie Moyer**, *pitcher, Seattle Mariners.*
> *Sellersville, Pennsylvania. All-star.*

"You learn to tune it out. I feel I've earned my spot. So for anybody else to say anything, they're not the ones who gave me the chance to play. I think at first it does affect you. You're thinking, 'Why the heck is this person on me so much?' At the same time you just kind of tune it out and feel confident and be confident knowing that you're good enough. If you let the (negative) affect you, then you are not preparing yourself to be able to do your job."

> **Russ Ortiz**, *pitcher, Atlanta Braves.*
> *Encino, California. All-star.*

TAKING STEPS

"They are trying to get you thinking about something other than baseball."

—DEAN PALMER

"That can be tough. Sometimes people say a lot of negative things, a lot of personal things and it can get under your skin a little bit. They are trying to get you thinking about something other than baseball. I've learned that they really don't know you. They're just there to try to get you off your game. You just have to be confident and know that what they're trying to do is nothing really personal."

Dean Palmer, *infielder, Detroit Tigers. Tallahassee, Florida. All-star.*

"They're doing it for a reason. You can put a positive spin on it and say, 'I'm in this position that somebody can tease me'. That's the way I look at it. Sometimes it's kind of funny to listen to what they have to say. And sometimes people say things that are out of line. But you just got to blow it off. You can't really worry about it."

Josh Phelps, *infielder, Toronto Blue Jays. Anchorage, Alaska.*

"It's tough. It's something you have to be able to block out. I continually make those mental efforts to stay in the game. 'What's the situation? What am I going to do when the ball is hit to me'? That will help me get out of whatever it is they're saying. You don't have to turn and acknowledge them because that tends to spurn more of it. Sometimes you can laugh with them. Don't take yourself too seriously."

Tim Salmon, *outfielder, Anaheim Angels. Long Beach, California. AL Rookie of the Year, 1993. World Series Champion, 2002.*

"Just take it. You just sit there and listen to them. Anything that can go on in our business, that can take you off of what you are doing, the other person has been successful. I am a big person to let character stand the test of time."

John Smoltz, *pitcher, Atlanta Braves. Detroit, Michigan. World Series Champion, 1995. NL Cy Young Award Winner, 1996. NL Rolaids Relief Winner, 2002. 6-time All-star.*

"If somebody is attacking me as a person, I close my eyes immediately and say, 'God, give me strength to get through this and not act in a way like he's acting.' I think name calling and picking on kids is something that is usually brought on by peer pressure. (It's) guys who want to be cool in front of other friends or try to chop off someone's head to make them look taller. But a real cool kid encourages his teammates to be better, makes his teammates feel good about themselves. That's what is necessary to have a winning team."

Mike Sweeney, *infielder, Kansas City Royals. Orange, California. 4-time All-star.*

"(The fans) can say anything they want. But if you're going to believe that, you're going to be in serious problems, because they're going to keep going and going. But if you take it like, 'Okay. Fine. Yes,' sometimes the fans get tired because you're (not responding to them). They try to get you mad. If you get mad, you're doing them a favor, because they'll keep going. But if you don't care, they'll try to pick on another player. That's the little things you have to learn about the fans."

Fernando Valenzuela, *former pitcher (ML career, 1980-1997), Los Angeles Dodger, California Angels, Baltimore Orioles, Philadelphia Phillies, San Diego Padres. Navojoa, Mexico. Rookie of the Year, 1981. NL Cy Young Award Winner, 1981. Gold Glove Winner. 6-time All-star.*

"You have to force yourself to ignore it. I have learned, as I got older, that a lot of people base their self-worth on what other people think about you. It's really not the way to do it. You have to be happy with yourself. You have to be confident in yourself. A lot of that stems from the way you were brought up, from your parents and your friends. The society that we live in today, a lot of people place everybody's self-worth on how much money they make or how successful they are in their jobs. I think my self-worth is based on the type of person that I am, not what I do on the field."

Tim Wakefield, *pitcher, Boston Red Sox. Melbourne, Florida.*

"I realized that if people are calling me names, it's either in fun, which most times it is here, so it's funny, but if there's some type of malicious intent, I just rise above it. I kind of let it bead off me like water. I realize that the people that are doing the name-calling are the ones truly hurting. They're the ones that are truly struggling inside."

Barry Zito, *pitcher, Oakland Athletics. Las Vegas Nevada. AL Cy Young Award Winner, 2002. 2-time All-star.*

Step up to the challenge:

- Which Big Leaguer's advice about dealing with hecklers did you like best?
- In your opinion, what's the point in teasing someone?
- What are some positive things you can say to yourself when someone is putting you down?

 ## Step out of the box to look for the signs

Try this for a week: As you go about your day, start to notice how you react when people insult you or say things that don't sit right with you. What's the feeling that comes up when you hear those words? What is a positive way for you to handle it?

The Error Monster!

"I don't reflect upon myself as a poor player,
just a player that had a poor performance."

—GREGG ZAUN

They happen almost every game. Everybody sees
them. And they never feel good when they happen, especially when you're involved—ERRORS!!
They're like monsters in a horror movie, there's no
avoiding them.

On and off the field, we make errors or mistakes
in all areas of our lives. In school, taking a test is like
playing in a baseball game. Both the school test and

baseball game are "testing" you to see how good you are, that day. We all want to do well and sometimes when we don't, we can get down on ourselves. Nobody is perfect.

Believe it or not, many of the players I spoke with feel the same way you do when they make an error—and they're not happy about it either. It doesn't make it any easier when it happens in front of a lot of people who are counting on you or there to watch you play.

So how do you deal with this "Error Monster" when it rears its ugly head? When I spoke with the ball players, the four main areas that came up about dealing with errors are what I titled: Preparation, Acceptance, Controlling Your Emotions, and Staying Positive.

Working on all four of these will help you build confidence for those games and tests.

ACCEPTANCE

"It's just like making a wrong turn in a car, you just turn back around and keep going. I just go out there and try to do the best I can. If I make a mistake I just try to make the next play. It's pretty simple. You are expected to do the majority of things right. If you mess up one time that doesn't mean that the whole day is a loss."

Jim Edmonds, *outfielder, St. Louis Cardinals. Fullerton, California. 6-time Gold glove Winner. 3-time All-star.*

"Errors are tough. I admit it. Last night I had a ball hit off my head. That's pretty embarrassing. You just got to tell yourself that it's over with. Let's do this for the team. Let's go out there and get those last couple of outs for the team and get back in the dugout. If you just have the mindset of putting the team ahead of yourself and go out there and do your job, you'll be okay."

Jay Gibbons, *outfielder, Baltimore Orioles. Rochester, Mississippi.*

"It is tough. You have to forget about it. You can't have it in the back of your mind, but everyone does. You drop an easy fly ball, a ball you catch a hundred times in a row in practice without even thinking about it. All of a sudden the next fly ball you're thinking, 'Oh my God, is this going to fall out of my glove?' It happens. Major Leaguers feel the exact same way kids do. No matter how good you are, you still have that same doubtful feeling in your stomach. Everyone goes through that so don't feel like you're the only one feeling that way. The more passive you are, the more errors you're going to make. The next ball that comes to you, don't wait for it, go right after it."

Ben Grieve, *outfielder, Tampa Bay Devil Rays. Arlington, Texas. AL Rookie of the Year, 1998. All-star.*

"Forget about it. Believe that you're going to make the next play. You can't go back. Just concentrate on the next one. When the ball's hit to you, then you make that play. You're going to do more good for your team than bad. If you make an error—so what, move on. You may work on it the next day, but go out there and have some fun."

Ken Griffey Jr., *outfielder, Cincinnati Reds. Donora, Pennsylvania. 10-time Gold Glove Winner. AL MVP, 1997. 11-time All-Star.*

"The most important thing is to simplify things down to making one pitch or just seeing the ball and hitting the ball. That's it. Sometimes if you give up a couple of runs, it's hard to relax and get back to that point. It's important for me to remember that no matter how much I want to, I can't change anything that has already happened. I can't control the future, I can't control past. Really, the only thing I can control is what I'm doing at that very second. And that is my focus. I'm going to try and control this next pitch. After that, I don't know what I'm going to do. I'm just going to concentrate on that."

Roy Halladay, *pitcher, Toronto Blue Jays. Denver, Colorado. Cy Young Award Winner, 2003. 2-time All-star.*

TAKING STEPS

*"Errors are tough. I admit it.
Last night I had a ball
hit off my head."*

—JAY GIBBONS

"The best fielder in the world makes errors. Don't look at the error a player just made, look at how he reacts to it. Look at how professional he is about it on the next ball he gets. He goes about it just like he always does. It's the same ground ball you've done a million times. Is he determined to make up for his mistake? Or did he go into a shell? They are still the same guy they were before that (error). You think, 'All right, I'll get 'em the next time.' "

Doug Mientkiewicz, *infielder, Minnesota Twins. Toledo, Ohio. Gold Glove Winner.*

"It is really tough, actually. Especially being a catcher. I think the team reflects its catcher. There really is no answer on how to (deal with an error). You just have to say, 'OK, now this is my job.' There's really no way of knowing how to do it. You just do it. You have to in order to be a successful catcher."

Damian Miller, *catcher, Chicago Cubs. LaCrosse, Wisconsin. World Series Champion, 2001. All-star.*

"The people I'm playing against are competing just as hard as I am to get a base hit, to get on base or to score a run, whatever the case. I think everybody playing this game has to realize that. The guy you're pitching against, or the guy who is pitching to you is trying to do the same thing you are doing—to try and succeed. Somebody's going to succeed and somebody's going to fail. Whether you succeed or don't, you have to go out and throw the next pitch or take that next at-bat and keep going. If you keep going at it, eventually it comes around and you get your piece of success too. There is a lot to learn from failing seven times out of ten and still being a success. Errors are part of the game. You have to go out and experience and learn for yourself."

Mike Mussina, *pitcher, New York Yankees. Williamsport, Pennsylvania. 6-time Gold Glove Winner. 5-time All-star.*

TAKING STEPS

"Errors are part of the game. You have to go out and experience and learn for yourself."

—MIKE MUSSINA

"You have to accept it and move on. You made a mistake and you try to learn from it. You ask yourself what you should have done differently or if you could have done anything differently. If you can learn from that and move on, then the error is no longer really a failure. You've learned from it and have turned it into a positive. It's a learning experience. Everything should be. You should always ask yourself those questions, whether in baseball or in life. 'Is there something I could've done different?' If not. Let it go."

Josh Phelps, *infielder, Toronto Blue Jays.*
Anchorage, Alaska.

"There is more than one aspect of the game to do, whether it be throwing a guy out, making a great catch or making a slide to break up a double play to keep the inning alive. There are a lot of things that go into this game that I feel, when one thing is not going well, you can contribute another way. To walk back to the dugout because the guy struck you out is just part of life. You better get used to it. There are going to be a lot more days like it."

Larry Walker, *outfielder, Colorado Rockies.*
Maple Ridge, British Columbia, Canada.
7-time Gold Glove Winner. NL MVP 1997.
5-time All-star.

TAKING STEPS

"I just said, 'You know what, let's go back out and have fun . . .'"

—JARROD WASHBURN

"The most important thing I have learned in all my years of pitching is how to deal with failure and not let it affect me into the next pitch, next batter or the next game. I learned that in Double-A ball in Midland, Texas. Every start I'd do worse and I'd take it into the next start. I was mentally beating myself up. Finally I just said, 'You know what, let's go back out and have fun—do what I've always loved doing and just have fun playing the game. If I give up a home run, if I have a bad game, I can't go back and change it so there's no sense in getting mad'. Now I've become really good at being able to discard any negative thoughts on the mound. If I make a bad pitch and give up a home run, I don't mentally beat myself up any more because I can't change it. That's helped me move forward with it. You're going to fail more than you achieve your goal in this game. Being able to deal with the failures is one of the most important parts of being successful."

Jarrod Washburn, *pitcher, Anaheim Angels. LaCrosse, Wisconsin. World Series Champion, 2002.*

ADJUSTMENTS.

"Baseball is a game of concentration and repetition. You always move forward. What's the next play? The next moment is always what's important. Once a moment is over, you have to go to the next moment. That's how the game works. Your concentration level has to be kept high for the whole game. That's how I forget about errors. I'm worried about the next moment already. For me to succeed, I have to be 100% focused on what's going to happen, not what has happened. I always look forward."

> **Craig Counsell**, *infielder, Arizona Diamondbacks. South Bend, Indiana. World Series Champion, 1997.*

"I am a big visualizer. I visualize every pitch before I throw it. I try to visualize (the type of pitch) and the location I want. If you train your mind to be positive and visualize that positive pitch, it's amazing how many times that happens, where the results turn out the way you want them to. I visualize myself going through the motion and making that pitch. It's just a split second thing you can do. It reinforces the positive thing in your brain saying, 'Okay here's the pitch I'm going to make', instead of, 'I can't give up a home run here.' I guarantee if you talk to anyone in this room, they've done that. Not every pitch is going to be perfect. Not every out is going to be perfect. You have to somehow move on."

> **Chad Fox,** *pitcher, Boston Red Sox, Florida Marlins. Houston, Texas. World Series Champion, 2003.*

"It's tough. Coach Adams (from) UCLA always told me that baseball is a game of quick recovery. Even if you drop a ball, you still got to make a play and try to throw the guy out—as opposed to just dropping the ball, getting upset that you missed the ball and then don't finish the play out. The people that can recover quicker and can limit their mistakes are also the people that are the best."

Dave Roberts, *outfielder, Los Angeles Dodgers. Okinawa, Japan.*

"If I give up a home run, walk a batter or give up a base hit, I just try to make an adjustment. I figure out what I can do to make the pitch much better. I take every pitch like a photo. I see the picture in my mind before and then say, 'Okay, I want the pitch, for example, on the outside corner on right-handed hitter.' In my mind, I have some pitch that I remember that I like and I just try to do the same thing."

Francisco Rodriguez, pitcher, Anaheim Angels. Caracas, Venezuela. World Series Champion, 2002.

"The biggest thing is to think about whatever situation is coming up. Before I actually do what I need to do during that play, I take a nice deep breath and clear my mind. A lot of times, I'll repeat something in my head to not allow anything else in. So if I'm going to make a pitch, I'll just say, 'Glove, glove, glove' to myself to get to the catcher's glove rather than think about what the coaches are thinking or anything going on in the stands. It helps me keep focused.

Steve Sparks, *pitcher, Detroit Tigers.*
Tulsa, Oklahoma.

CONTROL EMOTIONS

"I say to myself, 'There's nothing I can do about it now, it's over with.' The negativity (you feel) from that error is only going to make things worse. I might make another error because now I'm not focused on what I need to focus on. Sometimes I'll smooth the dirt out or take my glove off for a second and take a deep breath and get back into the moment of what I'm trying to do. They say give yourself (a few) seconds of getting angry, and then you got to move on."

Sean Casey, *infielder, Cincinnati Reds.*
Willingboro, New Jersey. 2-time All-Star.

TAKING STEPS

"The negativity (you feel) from that error is only going to make things worse."

—SEAN CASEY

"I do a lot of mental training stuff. Before the game, I always look at one point, like a flag or some advertising signs. When you see the flag, you remind yourself and say, 'This is just baseball. Don't be too serious. Okay, back to baseball. Now I can pitch.' Also, I use deep breaths and that helps even if I don't give up any (runs). I use it as a routine. If you give up something, walk off the mound, look at the flag and take a few deep breaths and then come back to the mound. A lot of guys do that."

Shigetoshi Hasegawa, *pitcher, Seattle Mariners. Kobe, Japan. All-star.*

"There is a little routine that a lot of big leaguers go through in between pitches. You see a little clump in the dirt to smooth over that means, 'Okay, I'm starting over, clean the slate', like you would a chalkboard. Erase it. There are times when I find myself getting really tense, and feeling the pressure of the game. I just take a deep breath. It helps you relax. It helps everything slow down. When the nerves start going, the game starts speeding up. The guy who the game comes easy to thinks it's slow. But the guy who is struggling thinks the guy pitching is throwing a hundred miles an hour."

> **Joe Lawrence**, *catcher, Milwaukee Brewers. Lake Charles, Louisiana.*

"It's just a matter of going through the process. Things happen. You can breathe through it. A lot of times you try the best you can to clear your mind, focus and breathe. Obviously when you are struggling you want to be around guys that you respect that will keep you positive. I get up there and I take a couple of deep breaths nice and slow to try to slow my heartbeat down a little bit. I do the same in the on-deck circle. I do the same even when I'm catching to try to relax. That's something that I've done over the years. I've taken yoga in the past so that's helped me to get back to that state of mind you want to be in when you are going well."

> **Mike Lieberthal**, *catcher, Philadelphia Phillies. Glendale, California. Gold Glove Winner. 2-time All-star.*

"The process is very simple. You never throw a pitch while you are angry about the last pitch. Sometimes it takes one second, sometimes it takes 30 seconds or it might take a minute. I think the process is to recognize when you are no longer upset about the last pitch you've thrown and then start to throw your next one. (You can) kick the grass, throw the rosin bag or give yourself a pep talk, whatever it is. Each day is different. It's very important to me not to have the last pitch on my mind as I'm throwing my next pitch."

> **Greg Maddux,** *pitcher, Atlanta Braves.*
> *San Angelo, Texas. 4-time Cy Young*
> *Award Winner. 13-time Gold Glove Winner.*
> *World Series Champion, 1995. 8-time All-Star.*

"Being a catcher is one of the tougher positions, because you are definitely going to be involved in the next play. I have always used deep breaths, taking my mask off to refocus. When my mask is on I'm 100% focused on what I'm doing. Positive thoughts are absolutely strengthening. You have to go to what you did well and not dwell on what you did wrong because you are going to make mistakes. And every guy in here is going to screw up at some time. This game is about dealing with failure and rising above that. For me it's always through work. 'I've been there before. I have dealt with this situation. I know I can work through this', is the thought process that goes through my head. I have a focal point at each stadium

I go to when stuff goes wrong. It reminds me, 'I am good at this. I am good at this, I am good at what I do. This is something I can do'. It pumps yourself back up."

> **Chad Moeller**, *catcher, Arizona Diamondbacks. Upland, California.*

"Don't think about it anymore. You know what you did when you made the error. Turn around and take your hat off and get your mind right and know what you need to do differently. 'Okay, now the ball was hit here make sure I stay down.' Just exaggerate things like you would if you were in practice. It gives you that confidence that the next ball hit to you, you'll catch it. But if you get scared because maybe the fans start booing and they get on you, just take your time."

> **Jimmy Rollins**, *infielder, Philadelphia Phillies. Oakland California. 2-time All-star.*

TAKING STEPS

"I have a focal point at each stadium I go to when stuff goes wrong. It reminds me, 'I am good at this.'"

—CHAD MOELLER

STAYING POSITIVE

"No matter what kind of ugly jam you're in out there, you're always just one pitch away from getting out of it. I try to think of the major surgery that I had. If I need to, I'll step off the rubber and take a peek of my scar and realize I was almost done pitching. It puts things in perspective. For me, it's a positive way to look at things and say, 'Make your pitch.' I have already been through tougher than this."

Jason Bere, *pitcher, Cleveland Indians. Cambridge, Massachusetts. All-star.*

"It's really tough to do. Talking to older players when I was coming up said, 'Listen, you got to take that play out of your head and just totally try to forget about it.' It's easier said than done, but just continue to say to yourself, 'I'm the best player on the field. I can make every single play.'"

Frank Catalanotto, *outfielder, Toronto Blue Jays. Smithtown, New York.*

"There's nothing I can do about it now, it is already over with. What can I do to get us out of that situation that we are in? What am I going to do now when the ball is hit to me? If you focus on the negative, it's going to affect you for the next play. A lot of times I'm seeing how the pitchers are pitching and I'm riding the wave with them. They get into a tight situation I'll find myself stressing out with them. It just clicked in my head one day. I said, 'Why am I worried about this? We are already in that situation, how are we going to get out of it?' You focus on the next play, not what has already happened. It kind of takes your mind off of what you just did."

Steve Finley, *outfielder, Arizona Diamondbacks. Paducah, New York 4-time Gold Glove Winner. World Series Champion, 2001. 2-time All-star.*

"Every time I'm on the mound, I try to think about positive stuff. I think, 'What did I feel when I struck out Ken Griffey Jr., Mark McGwire (ML career, 1986–2001), Sammy Sosa, the big guys I used to look up to?' Like Mark McGwire, I struck him out in St. Louis a couple of years ago—that stuck in my head. That's a positive picture in my head. Anytime anything goes bad, I try to go back to the positive side. I think, 'Okay, I struck out that guy, that guy, and that guy. I'm pretty good, even though I gave up a home run.' You just have to go back to your comfort level, your comfort zone, where it's all positive. You try to slow down everything. You try to picture in your head a positive. You try to picture a strike out. You try to picture a ground ball. Whatever you need. And that's what I try to do every time, every pitch."

Eric Gagne, *pitcher, Los Angeles Dodgers. Montreal, Petit-Quebec, Canada. Cy Young Award Winner, 2003. Rolaids Relief Winner, 2003. 2-time All-star.*

TAKING STEPS

*"Whatever you are thinking
will help you relax or
make you tense."*

—EDGAR MARTINEZ

"After I get angry about what I've done, the first thing I say is, 'More opportunities like that are going to come'. So every time I make a mistake, rather than have a negative thought, I just learn from that. I try to get better the next time that situation happens. You have to think there are going to be a lot more opportunities for you to make it up."

Javy Lopez, *catcher, Atlanta Braves. Ponce, Puerto Rico. World Series Champion, 1995. 3-time All-star.*

"The toughest part of the game is to learn how to deal with adversity. Simple things that are positive that you can tell yourself, are very, very important. Just change the negative for a positive thought. Slowly you can learn and be aware when that happens. Then, when it does happen you can talk to yourself in a positive way—you're ready for the next ground ball or the next at-bat. Whatever you are thinking will help you relax or make you tense."

Edgar Martinez, *infielder, Seattle Mariners. New York, New York. 7-time All-star.*

"I want to stop this rally right now. So I put all my focus on the hitter that is coming up to the plate next. It's tough to focus sometimes. It's easy to say that I go out there and I stay focused for nine innings or however long you're out there, but there are times when you lose a little bit. Some guys don't know what to focus on and you try to figure that out. It all comes with a lot of trial and error. I try to focus on the very next pitch I'm going to make. Before I get on the rubber, I try to picture that pitch in my mind. And then when I get on the rubber, I just forget about it and throw the pitch. That seems to help me out a lot."

Kevin Milwood, *pitcher, Philadelphia Phillies. Gastonia, North Carolina. All-star.*

"That is a learned environment. You have to go out there and get beat so many times before you learn there's going to be a tomorrow. There's going to be a next pitch. I don't think you can just hear it from somebody and learn it. You have to go out and experience failure before you know how to handle failure."

Troy Percival, *pitcher, Anaheim Angels. Fontana, California. World Series Champion, 2002. 4-time All-star.*

"The most important thing is what your thoughts are five seconds after you've done something wrong. If you can rehash it, re-visualize it, and make it happen the way you want it to happen, then you're ready for the next ground ball. It is very essential that you don't think something negative because that carries on to something worse."

Alex Rodriguez, *infielder, Texas Ranger.*
New York, New York. 2-time Gold Glove
Winner. AL MVP 2003. 7-time All-star.

"People say they want the next ball hit to them. As a kid you say, 'If I get another one, I might make an error'. You need to reverse that thought and say, 'All right, if the next ball is hit to me, I'm going to make the play'. That's something that even professionals go through. If you make an error, that's a big thing. Personally, I visualize the ball coming toward me and making a play. I visualize catching it and throwing it, because you want to focus on the good and recreate the muscle memory and those good habits. If you create those good habits, they're more likely to continue to happen."

Mark Teixeira, *infielder, Texas Rangers.*
Severna Park, Maryland.

"Once you've given up the home run or you've walked the guy, you can't take it back. All you can do is put it behind you and try to work on the next guy. Getting too excited or trying to overdo it tends to get people in trouble, rather than trusting whatever it was that was getting the guys out with the previous pitches is the same thing that is going to get the next guy out. Just knowing that 70 percent of the time they're going to get out even if they are a good hitter. You can't go out there thinking of negative things. You have to find positive things to draw from. You may have thrown a ball, but maybe it was a good pitch and he didn't call it. Say things that are going to produce productivity and not negativity. You just got to stay positive and continue to convince yourself that if you execute what you're trying to do, more often then not, you're going to have success."

Kip Wells, *pitcher, Pittsburgh Pirates.*
Houston Texas.

"I just tell myself over and over again, 'You'll get the next one'. I don't reflect upon myself as a poor player, just a player that had a poor performance. I always try to talk positively to myself and my teammates. If you're a positive person and you're generally a happy person—people pick up on that."

Gregg Zaun, *catcher, Colorado Rockies.*
Glendale, California.

Step up to the challenge:

- Which big leaguer's advice on dealing with the "Error Monster" are you going to try the next time you make an error or mistake?
- What encouraging words would you like to hear from your teammates or coaches right after you made an error?
- What things can you do to remind yourself to pay attention during games and practice?

 ## Step out of the box to look for the signs

Try this for a week: As you go about your day, start to notice what you say to yourself when you make a mistake. Imagine if you were a Major League ball player, what would you say to a Little League kid to help him move past a mistake?

Success Secrets
To The Game

*"Focus on the things that create
the result, not the result."*

—DAMION EASLEY, advice from Alan Trammel

When someone tells you a secret, they're letting you into their private treasure chest of knowledge and information that perhaps only a few know about. And that information can be valuable to those who are willing to listen and use it.

Players share secrets and informational tips with each other all the time. They want to learn as much as they can about the other team so they can be successful when playing against them. The more information you gather to educate yourself, the greater your advantage. It's like being in charge of your own all-star team—you feel more confident about your options and choices.

Great information doesn't have to be a secret. It can come in the form of a book you read or advice you hear from a teacher, parent or friend. No matter where the information comes from, it's there to help you improve your skills and become a better player and person.

In the following pages, you have access to valuable information and tips on what it takes for these Big Leaguers to be successful, overcome challenges and stay on top of their game. As you read this chapter, look for ways to apply these success secrets to all areas of your life.

TAKING STEPS

*"You got to have a thought.
You got to have a plan."*

—CRAIG BIGGIO

"Chris Bando (ML career, 1981–1989) was my manager in Double-A. The best advice he ever gave me was a little acronym called, ACE—Attitude. Concentration. Effort. He said that those are the things that you can control every game. Prepare yourself, and keep a consistent attitude of trying to put others before yourself. Concentrate on your game plan and give it your best effort."

Josh Bard, *catcher, Cleveland Indians.*
Ithaca, New York.

"K.I.S.S. Keep It Simple Stupid. It's a very difficult game. You got to have a thought. You got to have a plan. You got to have an idea. The simpler you keep it, the easier the game is going to be. But you still got to have an idea of what you want to do."

Craig Biggio, *outfielder, Houston Astros.*
Smithtown, New York. 4-time Gold Glove
Winner. 7-time All-Star.

"Work hard and respect the game. Treat people how you want to be treated. I think that it comes from my father. He played for 15 years because of what he did on and off the field. He treated people how he wanted to be treated. He never disrespected the game. He played hard and left it all on the field."

Sean Burroughs, *infielder, San Diego*
Padres. Atlanta, Georgia.

"It doesn't take any talent to hustle. It doesn't matter how good you are, it doesn't take any talent to play the game right, to play the game hard. My dad was really big on that."

Sean Casey, *infielder, Cincinnati Reds.*
Willingboro, New Jersey. 2-time All-Star.

"You learn things by watching how other quality people carry themselves. The best thing you can learn in anything is a work ethic. There's no substitute for hard work."

Craig Counsell, *infielder, Arizona*
Diamondbacks. South Bend, Indiana.
World Series Champion, 1997, 2001.

"I asked Alan Trammel (ML career, 1977–1996) how he was able to be so consistent for so long. He said simply that good day or bad day, he makes sure he follows his routine. He stays focused on the things that create the result, not the result—the process. I've always taken heart to that, to make sure that on and off the field, I do the things that I believe in that are right, that's going to make me a complete person.

Damion Easley, *infielder, Detroit Tigers.*
New York, New York. All-Star.

"Baseball is going to be here and it's going to be gone tomorrow, but the way people perceive you is going to be there forever. I grew up with Bruce Sutter (ML career, 1976-1988). He always told me, 'Go out there

TAKING STEPS

". . . have fun. Don't make it a life-and-death situation. This is just a game."

—JOHN FRANCO

and play hard every day and don't sell yourself short'. I try to play hard every day and just be myself and not try to do too much. I don't try to be somebody I'm not, but go out there and be Adam."

Adam Everett, *infielder, Houston Astros. Austell, Georgia.*

"I try to go out and have fun. Don't make it a life-and-death situation. This is just a game. Yes, everybody wants to win, but somebody has to lose also. Losing is part of the game. And I think losing builds character too. When it's a tough situation, I know that I've been in that situation before and I know that I have the ability to get out of it. So I try not to get too caught up in the moment. I just try to maintain my concentration level and make good quality pitches and get out of the situation.

John Franco, *pitcher, New York Mets. Brooklyn, New York. NL Rolaids Relief Winner, 1988, 1990. 4-time All-Star.*

"The biggest thing is work hard. Never lose sight of your dreams and keep chasing them. You're the person who has the last say, not everybody else. My brother and I are living our dreams right now. My dad said a lot of that advice. Mark McGwire took me under his wing when I first got to the Big Leagues. He taught me a lot about the game and how to approach it. He was a big influence on my career."

Jason Giambi, *infielder, New York Yankees. West Covina, California. AL MVP, 2000. 4-time All-star.*

"Have fun and play hard. Those are the two qualities that have nothing to do with physical ability or physical talent. You can always have fun and you can always play hard."

Troy Glaus, *infielder, Anaheim Angels. Tarzana, California. World Series Champion, 2002. World Series MVP, 2002. 2-time All-Star.*

"My dad was the person I wanted to be like growing up. He said, 'You're not me. Don't imitate anybody. Just be yourself'. Go out there and have some fun and be yourself. Be true to yourself."

Ken Griffey Jr., *outfielder, Cincinnati Reds. Donora, Pennsylvania. 10-time Gold Glove Winner. AL MVP, 1997. 11-time All-Star.*

"You're not as good as they say you are, and you're not as bad as they say you are. So that really takes everything out of the equation. So go out there and play the game and you'll be happy with what you're doing. Ultimately, it comes down to who you are and what you feel about yourself."

Jeffrey Hammonds, *outfield, Milwaukee Brewers. Plainfield, New Jersey. All-star.*

"Two words, 'What if?' Never leave yourself with the question, 'What if?' What if I had tried a little harder? What if I had spent a little more time studying my craft? It's pretty simple. What if I tried a little harder at school? What if I had gotten along a little bit better with others? What if I had respected my parents a little more? It's pretty important stuff, I think."

Trevor Hoffman, *pitcher, San Diego Padres. Bellflower, California. Rolaids Relief Award Winner. 4-time All-star.*

TAKING STEPS

"Be patient. Patience is the key.
You will be rewarded . . ."

—TORII HUNTER

"My parents told me no matter how far you may get in this game, you're still no better than nobody else. The Lord blessed you with this talent to play this game, you keep your head level. There's going to be some ups and downs in this game all the time. It's a hard game. You just go out and have fun and thank the Lord every day after (you go) 0-4 or 4-4. You give Him the lift and the praise and tell Him thanks.

Orlando Hudson, *infielder, Toronto Blue Jays. Darlington, South Carolina.*

"One of the things that Kirby Puckett, (Hall of Fame, 2001) and Dave Winfield, (Hall of Fame, 2001) always said, 'It's going to be a long journey. Be patient.' Patience is the key. A lot of people want it fast. That's what I wanted as a young guy. It's not going to work out when you want it, but it will be there. You will be rewarded when you get it. You have to go through struggle to have progress. That's what I did and that's what most of these players did in here.

Torii Hunter, *outfielder, Minnesota Twins. Pine Bluff, Arkansas. 3-time Gold Glove Winner. All-Star.*

TAKING STEPS

"Anything is possible if you decide what it is you want."

—RAFAEL PALMEIRO

"Try not to take a bad step when you're on the field. I think that meant walking to your position, or not making the full play—sort of cutting it short and making a bad step. Make every step be a good step, something positive. That will keep you sharp."

Tom Kelly, *former manager, 1986-2001, Minnesota Twins. Graceville, Minnesota. AL Manager of the Year, 1991. World Series Champion, 1987, 1991.*

"From a baseball standpoint, I think Tony Perez (Hall of Fame, 2000) was extremely instrumental in my early playing career. He told me to keep my eyes and ears open and my mouth closed. He told me I could learn a lot by watching. I try to learn, obviously, by my mistakes, but also by the mistakes of others that I see around me. I just try not to make the same mistakes that the people who went before me made."

Barry Larkin, *infielder, Cincinnati Reds. Cincinnati, Ohio. 3-time Gold Glove Winner, NL MVP, 1995. World Series Champion, 1990. 11-time All-Star.*

"It all goes back to when I first started playing. I made a commitment to play a lot of games in the summer, which sacrificed a lot of the time we had as kids in the summer. The sacrifice put us on the baseball field and gave us the opportunity to improve and to learn a lot. We were exposed to good coaching, the game of baseball and people of other talents. The more exposed you are to the game, the better you're going to be."

Mike Matheny, *catcher, St. Louis Cardinals. Columbus, Ohio. 2-time Gold Glove Winner.*

"Anything is possible in life if you set your mind and heart (to it). As a young kid I heard a lot of people say, 'You're crazy. It's just a dream. It's not ever going to happen.' I wanted not just to do it for myself, but to prove all those people wrong. I always said, 'There are guys up there playing, why can I not be one of those?' I just told myself that I was going to do whatever it took. I was going to work hard. I was going to achieve my dream. It's all in what you want to do with yourself. Anything is possible if you decide what it is you want."

Rafael Palmeiro, *infielder, Baltimore Orioles. Havana, Cuba. 3-time Gold Glove Winner. 4-time All-star.*

"Baseball is a game where you have to learn to deal with failure a lot and not let it really get you down. That's the same thing in life. You don't want to be up and down, angry and mad. You just have to learn to let a lot of stuff roll off your back and go on with life. You have to learn from your mistakes and try to make yourself better in baseball and the same thing in life. When you get angry on the baseball field, it doesn't make you any better to show it. Take some deep breaths to regain your focus or regain your thoughts. You just have to realize every day, every game is not going to be successful. It builds character when you make it through those tough times."

Dean Palmer, *infielder, Detroit Tigers. Tallahassee, Florida. All-Star.*

"Never forget your roots. Never forget where you come from. When you're a little kid, you have people who love you, care for you and want you to succeed in the game you play. You always have to remember that. A lot of people, these days, make a lot of money in this game and they forget where they come from. They want to be a whole different person than who they are. I don't think that's nice. But everybody is different."

Sydney Ponson, *pitcher, Baltimore Orioles. Noord, Aruba.*

"Have your eyes and ears open and your mouth shut. If you get a chance to take the whole thing in and see what's happening around you, the game unfolds itself, if you just pay attention. If you're not shooting your mouth off trying to be seen and noticed, rather you notice and see what's going on around you, I think you can become a better ball player and a better person."

Scott Rolen, *infielder, St. Louis Cardinals. Evansville, Indiana. 5-time Gold Glove Winner. NL Rookie of the Year, 1997. 2-time All-Star.*

"Tough times don't last, tough people do. My dad told me that when I was a kid and it's something I've never forgotten."

Curt Schilling, *pitcher, Arizona Diamondbacks. Anchorage, Alaska. World Series Champion, 2001. World Series co-MVP, 2001. 5-time All-Star.*

TAKING STEPS

". . . believe that you belong here."

—OMAR VIZQUEL

"My dad was in athletics. The biggest thing that stood with me from him was that there is a right way and wrong way to do things. When I got to the big leagues Robin Yount (Hall of Fame, 1999. ML career, 1974–1993), who I learned a ton from, and other guys, said, 'You're not always going to do the right thing every day, but you should be trying to do the right thing.' Whether you're winning or losing, you should always be trying to do the right thing at the right time and play the game right away."

B. J. Surhoff, *outfielder, Baltimore Orioles. Bronx, New York. All-Star.*

"It's not what you do when you walk in the door, it's what you do when you leave, the lasting impressions that you give and how you handle the bad times. It's easy to be happy when everything is going good. It's very similar to life. It's all about making adjustments in your life and understanding and having responsibility for everything you do. My parents were a big influence (as well as) my family and my wife."

Jim Thome, *infielder, Philadelphia, Phillies. Peoria, Illinois. 3-time All-Star.*

"The harder you work doesn't guarantee you that you're going to be successful in baseball. But I found, the harder you work the better chances you have. This game is not really fair. You can do everything perfect and still be out. It just teaches you to keep striving. It can really knock you to your knees, but you still get up and work hard and prepare."

Robin Ventura, *infielder, Los Angeles Dodgers. Santa Maria, California. 6-time Gold Glove Winner. 2-time All-Star.*

"Never give up no matter what other people say or think about you. If you really believe in yourself, you can accomplish a lot of things. In this game you have a lot of people telling you that you can't play—you are too small, you don't have a strong enough arm or you can't run. You have to forget about that and really push yourself and believe that you belong here."

Omar Vizquel, *infielder, Cleveland Indians. Caracas, Venezuela. 9-time Gold Glove Winner. 3-time All-Star.*

"A lot of people say, 'Keep your head up, no matter what you go through, good or bad.' Just as in life, you're going to go through adversity. Keep your head up, no matter if you're the worst player or the best player. That's just something I learned in life from losing a lot of games, a lot of big games. It teaches you class."

Dontrelle Willis, *pitcher, Florida Marlins. Alameda, California. NL Rookie of the Year, 2003. World Series Champion, 2003. All-star.*

"You learn how to deal with adversity and keep going. Life is about adversity, problems and overcoming them. And that's kind of what baseball is. Even when you are good, you fail a lot. And if you know how to handle that, you will be pretty good in life."

Dave Winfield, *Hall of Fame 2001, outfielder, (ML career, 1973-1995) San Diego Padres, New York Yankees, California Angeles, Toronto Blue Jays, Minnesota Twins, Cleveland Indians. St. Paul, Minnesota. 7-time Gold Glove Winner. World Series Champion, 1992. 12-time All-Star.*

"You have to go out there and set goals for yourself, however small. Try to achieve those goals and never give up. Always keep going because when you're going back to the dugout seven times out of ten, you learn to deal with failure and adversity. You learn it's one of those things that's going to happen in life too. You have to keep a positive attitude or you won't be successful.

You're the only one that can tell you that you can't do it. If you go out there with the attitude that you can succeed and nobody's going to stop you, more often than not you'll be successful."

Gregg Zaun, *catcher, Colorado Rockies. Glendale, California.*

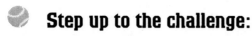

Step up to the challenge:

- Which player's success secrets do you think will best help you in baseball? In school? At home? With your friends?
- Which success secrets have you heard before that weren't from a baseball player? Where did you hear them?
- What's the secret to YOUR success?

Step out of the box to look for the signs

Try this for a week: As you go about your day, start to notice other people's success. Ask them what their secret is to success. What are some of the things they do to be successful and how can you bring it into your life?

C H A P T E R

Signs Of A Champion

"You become a champion first mentally . . .
then the championship comes."

—ALEX RODRIGUEZ

As you probably know in baseball, the team to score the most runs in the game wins. The Most Valuable Player Award is given to the best player in each league. What if we never kept score? How would you know who the winner was? If they never handed out trophies, who would be the champion?

The point is: How can you tell if a person was a "winner" in a sport with which you aren't familiar? Do you think you could recognize if a person was a champion just by the way they walked down the street? I believe you could.

Champions definitely do things differently to set themselves apart from the rest. They work smarter and harder at becoming better at what they do. In their mind, they see and think of themselves in a certain way. Did you know the way you think and feel about yourself has a huge impact on how well you're able to do something or rebound from a setback? When your brain is pumping in bad or negative stuff in your head, it's tough to have great things happen.

Watch a champion and see how they learn from their mistakes. Instead of getting down on themselves, they look at an error as an opportunity to get better. They realize that there's more game to be played.

It's like when you take a test in school and you get a question wrong. You can't dwell on the one you got wrong; there are more questions on the test.

At any given time there are at least 750 baseball players in the world playing Major League Baseball. The players I talked with shared their thoughts on what it takes to be and feel like a champion at this high level. Read on to find out what they say and see are the signs of a champion. It may surprise you.

"He is selfless. He works hard. He's self-motivated. He's got passion for what he does. He loves it. He's always looking to get better. He's got his ears open, always listening for advice. He's not thinking that he knows everything. He's a winner. He does not make excuses. He takes responsibility for what he does and for his actions."

Sean Casey, *infielder, Cincinnati Reds. Willingboro, New Jersey. 2-time All-Star.*

"Everyone in this room deserves to be here because of their talent, but it's up to them mentally to determine how long they're going to stay here. Some guys get frustrated easily. They go away from their plan and they're out of the game in a couple of years because they don't know how to get back on track. I think the most important part is knowing how to adapt and keep a level head. A lot of times, I'll play the game in my head before I actually play it on the field. I'll mentally go over or visualize what (the pitcher's) going to pitch to me. I try to play everything in my head before I even get up there. It makes you very prepared."

Jeff Conine, *infielder, Baltimore Orioles. Tacoma, Washington. World Series Champion, 1997, 2003. 2-time All-star.*

"It's good work habits. Not afraid to ask questions. Look at the veteran guys at how they carry themselves and how they approach situations. I was fortunate enough when I came up with Cincinnati that one of the top relief pitchers in the game at the time was Tom Hume, (ML career, 1977-1987). I learned a lot from him about how to carry myself on the field and off the field."

John Franco, *pitcher, New York Mets.*
Brooklyn, New York. NL Rolaids Relief Winner,
1988, 1990. 4-time All-Star.

"A lot of people said (because) I'm French Canadian, there's no way in the world you're going to be a base-ball player. You don't want to listen to negative. You want to listen to people who are trying to help, people like my mom, my dad, and my brother. They always believed in me. My coaches always tried to help me even though, sometimes, it was hard. Sometimes they say stuff you don't want to hear. But they always try to help. Even though I'm in the major leagues, I try to get better and better every day. That's the way it should be in life. You can always be better."

Eric Gagne, *pitcher, Los Angeles Dodgers.*
Montreal, Petit-Quebec, Canada. Cy Young
Award Winner, 2003. Rolaids Relief Winner,
2003. 2-time All-star.

TAKING STEPS

"It all comes back to preparation . . ."
—BRIAN GILES

"The biggest thing I learned is that you can't be scared. If you make a mistake, you're man enough to admit to your mistakes and then you go on, just as you're a man enough to accept your responsibilities at what you succeeded. You always keep learning and never feel that you have everything figured out, because you can always learn and be better. There's always some part of your game that you can be better at."

Jason Giambi, *infielder, New York Yankees. West Covina, California. AL MVP, 2000. 4-time All-star.*

"It all comes back to preparation before the game, doing your normal routine. During the game, thinking of situations where you know where to throw the ball if the ball is hit to you. That's all a part of mental preparation. That'll get you through the times when you're a little sluggish."

Brian Giles, *outfielder, San Diego Padres. El Cajon, California. 2-time All-star.*

"There are certain traits that can increase your chances of winning because you have a championship attitude. I think it has a lot to do with your character. What good is it if you're winning a championship and you cheated to get there? That's not a champion. A champion is how they carry it, respect for others, the game, valuing other people's feelings. To me it's a lot deeper than just winning something."

Doug Glanville, *outfielder, Texas Rangers. Hackensack, New Jersey.*

"Sometimes I do some visualization: I sit in a quiet place before the game or even during the game. I kind of go through an at-bat or go through a play on the field where you are succeeding. Another thing I try to do is pay attention to the game. Probably two-thirds of the guys, even at this level, don't really pay attention. They don't really see what the pitcher is trying to do. If you really pay attention, you see things that are so obvious. I'll watch how pitchers want to get a hitter out when it's a crucial time. You can see what pitches they really rely on. You can watch the game and not really see all the details."

Shawn Green, *outfielder, Los Angeles Dodgers. Des Plaines, Illinois. Gold Glove Winner. 2-time All-star.*

"Ever since I can remember, I always felt like I could do anything I wanted to do, whether it be in school or sports. I don't know if it was something my parents told me, or how I was brought up, but I always felt that way. Baseball has just basically proven that, if I work hard enough at anything, and care about something as bad as I care about the game, I can do it."

Todd Helton, *infielder, Colorado Rockies. Knoxville, Tennessee. 2-time Gold Glove Winner. 4-time All-star.*

"Most people I come across that are champions, their attitudes are different than the guys who aren't. You've heard the phrase of somebody being a winner? The qualities they possess are just different. You can see that. It's their attitude—positive attitude. Their personality is out-going. They're not really concerned with themselves as much as their team."

Tim Hudson, *pitcher, Oakland Athletics. Columbus, Georgia. All-star.*

"He understands what he's playing for and what he wants to achieve. He's willing to give it his all and go beyond what he thought he could do."

Randy Johnson, *pitcher, Arizona Diamondbacks. Walnut Creek, California. 5-time Cy Young Award Winner. World Series Champion, 2001. 9-time All-star.*

"Baseball teaches you a discipline, how to recover from negative things and how to work together to achieve a goal. It teaches you to understand that life isn't always good things. There are times where you are going to struggle, and that working hard is important. I think the amount of work that you put in, it repays you and if you reach this level, it'll repay you more than twice. If you have the ability and you have that drive, I think you'd be shortchanging yourself if you didn't maximize your talent."

Mike Lowell, *infielder, Florida Marlins. San Juan, Puerto Rico. World Series Champion, 2003. 2-time All-star.*

"For me, it goes back to putting in your time when you commit yourself to something and sticking with a commitment. My parents always told me when I was getting started with baseball that if I got on a team, there was no quitting. There was no, not showing up for a practice when something else was more convenient. I learned a lot of lessons about teamwork, about sticking through tough times, and about overcoming some obstacles. I learned about trusting other people. I learned about how hard you can push yourself and how far you can push yourself in training and preparation. I think there's so many lessons that kids can learn that won't only make them better baseball players but make them successful in every walk of life."

Mike Matheny, *catcher, St. Louis Cardinals. Columbus, Ohio. 2-time Gold Glove Winner.*

"I have a few checkpoints every single day. It all starts at home. I'm a big and firm believer of imagery. At home, I'll use the imagery to play the day through before it happens, so when it happens, I'm not surprised by it. I am prepared for it. You see your ride to the ballpark. You see yourself getting dressed and starting your routine. Everything just falls into place. I am a firm believer in setting goals and having a strong routine that you're not going to deviate from—you're going to be prepared every day."

Joe McEwing, *utility player, New York Mets. Bristol, Pennsylvania.*

"Someone with a great mind, a person who's quiet. He knows he's very good. He knows he's the best. He doesn't say it. A guy who's humble, that's a champion to me, not the guy who's always talking about it and saying things about himself."

Bengie Molina, *catcher, Anaheim Angels. Rio Piedras, Puerto Rico. 2-time Gold Glove Winner. World Series Champion, 2002.*

TAKING STEPS

"I took that stubbornness of trying to do it all myself, to a stubbornness of paying attention to details."

—TERRY MULHOLLAND

"I've learned about myself, that I have good qualities and I have bad qualities. I've had to learn, especially when I was young, about being patient as an athlete. I was one of those guys who had a little bit of a temper. I had to learn to kind of slow my pace down where I could become more consistent, rather than have too many highs or too many lows. The whole time you're doing that, you're learning about how to deal with other people, about how to respect other people, how to appreciate the opportunities that are given to you along the way."

> **Paul Molitor**, *Hall of Fame 2003, infielder (ML career, 1978-1998), Milwaukee Brewers, Toronto Blue Jays, Minnesota Twins. St. Paul, Minnesota. World Series Champion, 1993. World Series MVP, 1993. 7-time All-star.*

"I can be very stubborn both positive and negative ways. When I was young, I wanted so badly to perform well that I was very single minded in playing the game. I had such a stubborn approach. I believed in working hard and the harder I worked, the better I thought I would be. I wasn't always that open to suggestions on how to play the game. To a fault, that stubbornness probably held me back as a young player. When I got into pro baseball, I realized that there are a lot of guys with a lot of experience in this game who are a whole lot better than I am. If I was going to get anywhere, I was going to have to open up more, take their advice and apply it—trial and error. I took that stubbornness of trying to do it all myself, to a stubbornness of paying attention to details."

Terry Mulholland, *pitcher, Cleveland Indians. Uniontown, Pennsylvania. All-star.*

"Never think that you are that much better than your opponent. The minute I start thinking, 'I'm a better pitcher than this guy is a hitter,' you're getting rocked. That's the way it is. The minute you get too confident out there, or too cocky saying, 'I'm way better than this team, they can't hit me,' they will. If I'm not learning something every day, I'm getting dumber. Every day I'm learning something. I don't have it figured out."

Mark Mulder, *pitcher, Oakland Athletics. South Holland, Illinois. All-star.*

"He's a good leader. A guy that has a plan. A guy that sets his goals very high. He's not afraid to go get them. You have to set goals. You have to lead the way. You have to have a plan and you have to execute the plan."

Rafael Palmeiro, *infielder, Baltimore Orioles. Havana, Cuba. 3-time Gold Glove Winner. 4-time All-star.*

"You don't have to have great stuff. I think if you have a big heart and if you're willing to put in the work, you can will your way to get some stuff done. I've been able to pitch up here, I think, with a lot of heart whenever I wasn't able to throw a hard fastball or have a great curveball that night. I think it has made me a stronger man and a stronger person with all the adversity, dealing with a lot of problems. It shows you can get through a lot of stuff that you didn't think you'd be able to."

Andy Pettitte, *pitcher, New York Yankees. Baton Rouge, Louisiana. World Series Champion, 1996, 1998, 1999, 2000. 2-time All-star.*

"Trust in your ability. You can talk yourself into or out of almost any situation. You can talk yourself into winning when you don't think you have the ability to win and you can talk yourself into losing when you do have the ability to win and be successful. So much of it is how you perceive yourself. If you like yourself, if you respect yourself, if you can look yourself in the mirror, and answer the questions, 'Have I worked as hard as I can, have I prepared myself as well as I can?' The confidence and trust go with that."

Bryan Price, *pitching coach, Seattle Mariners. San Francisco, California.*

"This is a sport you got to stay really disciplined every day. It's a long season. You got to be disciplined on making sure you get your work in. That's what it has taught me in life, staying disciplined in the classroom, staying disciplined money-wise or having discipline in your faith, going to church."

Mark Prior, *pitcher, Chicago Cubs.*
San Diego, California. All-star.

"There are a lot of guys I played with growing up that were better baseball players then I was. They didn't make it to the big leagues. I think it's a matter of work ethic. I think learning to play the game right and being a team player is very important. Doing the little things right, whether it be bunting, fielding, or being a student of the game, that's helped me get to where I am and not just sheer ability."

Dave Roberts, *outfielder, Los Angeles Dodgers. Okinawa, Japan.*

"A champion is someone who is complete, determined, resilient, nonstop. It's all about being resilient and building to be a champion. I think you become a champion first mentally, with everything you do, and then the championship comes. I don't think it's the other way around. I think sometimes we, as athletes, want everything a little bit too easy. You get an opportunity— you're ready for anything."

Alex Rodriguez, *infielder, Texas Ranger.*
New York, New York. 2-time Gold Glove
Winner. AL MVP 2003. 7-time All-star.

"A champion is someone who's not afraid to go out there and make mistakes. If you make a mistake, oh well, you have another chance to be the hero. Some people are very tentative in the world, not just the game itself, and are afraid of success. Well, you're going to have problems if you're poor, you're going to have problems if you're rich. You're going to have problems if you are successful or unsuccessful. So you might as well be the best you can be and see where that takes you. If you make a mistake, you learn from it and you keep on ticking."

Jimmy Rollins, *infielder, Philadelphia*
Phillies. Oakland California. 2-time All-star.

TAKING STEPS

"... it's what you do after you fail that makes champions', champions."

—SCOTT SULLIVAN

"The guys that work hard, don't give up, believe in themselves, that try to make other people all around them better—those guys persevere. Anybody can play this game when it's going good. How do you play when things are going bad? I think that's the key in anything in life. It's easy to be that person in the public eye when you are doing well, but when things aren't going good, what kind a person are you?"

Tim Salmon, *outfielder, Anaheim Angeles. Long Beach, California. AL Rookie of the Year, 1993. World Series Champion, 2002.*

"I think the most important thing is patience, discipline and learning how to be away from your family. It comes with a lot of help with my wife and the support of my kids. It's not just me. It takes a family. With the kids, it takes your parents to be behind you. I've got another team back home."

Reggie Sanders, *outfielder, Pittsburgh Pirates. Florence, South Carolina. World Series Champion, 2001. All-star.*

109

"This is not a game of just being on top all the time. You're going to get knocked down. This game has taught me through trials to never give up, overcome injuries, bad outings or what people think of you. It's knowing who I am as a person first (and) not be consumed as a baseball player, I'm not consumed with everything that this job or this game does to me."

John Smoltz, *pitcher, Atlanta Braves. Detroit, Michigan. World Series Champion, 1995. NL Cy Young Award Winner, 1996. NL Rolaids Relief Winner, 2002. 6-time All-star.*

"If you give 100% every time you step on the field, and you have done everything you can to prepare yourself, maybe lose a game or you don't have a good game—you do that enough times, you're going to be a champion not only in baseball, but in life probably. Baseball prepares you for so many things. I think if you're out playing and competing as hard as you can, then at the end of the day, you have no reason to hang your head."

J. T. Snow, *infielder, San Francisco Giants. Long Beach, California. 6-time Gold Glove Winner.*

TAKING STEPS

"*. . . if you don't believe what you have, then talent means nothing.*"

—FERNANDO VALENZUELA

"I think it has more to do than talent. It's a belief system. Four or five years ago, I knew that I could be a major-league pitcher but I did not believe it. That next year, I believed. I had some success in the big leagues with the Indians and I believed I was a major league pitcher. The second that you believe that you belong up here is the same time you're going to have success."

Justin Speier, *pitcher, Colorado Rockies.*
Walnut Creek, California.

"It's the ultimate desire to do what it takes to win a ballgame—the sacrifice, the hard work, the perseverance. Everybody goes through failures and everybody fails. It's not the fact that you fail, it's what you do after you fail that makes champions', champions."

Scott Sullivan, *pitcher, Cincinnati Reds.*
Tuscaloosa, Alabama.

"Win or lose (a champion) stands up for his actions. If you lose the game, you don't throw an excuse out. Stand and face it. If you win the game, do the same. A champion really won't take the credit for it 9 times out of 10. They'll give that away. They'll spread the wealth and face the blame."

Mike Timlin, *pitcher, Boston Red Sox.*
Midland, Texas. World Series Champion,
1992, 1993.

"To be successful in this game, you have to believe in yourself. The talent is there but if you don't believe what you have, then talent means nothing. The main thing is to believe in yourself."

Fernando Valenzuela, *former pitcher*
(ML career, 1980-1997), Los Angeles Dodgers,
California Angels, Baltimore Orioles,
Philadelphia Phillies, San Diego Padres.
Navojoa, Mexico. Rookie of the Year, 1981.
NL Cy Young Award Winner, 1981. Gold
Glove Winner. 6-time All-star.

"I am a pretty mentally strong person and I can prove a lot of people wrong. I know as a kid I was always good. I came from a real small town (Webster, Wisconsin). I always told people I was going to play in the major leagues and people always said, "Okay, keep going to school, too". But I proved a lot of people wrong. Where I come from, nobody gets to make it big. I think basically baseball's taught me that I can do anything I put my mind to."

Jarrod Washburn, *pitcher, Anaheim*
Angels. LaCrosse, Wisconsin. World Series
Champion, 2002.

"I think you're doing yourself a disservice by not paying attention as a pitcher, 'What did I do this outing good and what did I do this outing poorly? What do I need to try to concentrate on next time out?' You find out a lot about yourself by putting yourself in a situation to be successful. Maybe you're not in the game, but you're prepared that one time you get a chance to pinch-hit. Guys put themselves in situations to be successful, but it's only because of hard work and preparation that those things come out in your favor."

Kip Wells, *pitcher, Pittsburgh Pirates.*
Houston, Texas.

"Toughness, of the mind and the body—you got to have both. You got to have perseverance. You got to have that ability to make adjustments. I think that really helps. Also, you got to have pride in yourself to make sure that this is an important thing for you. You just can't throw yourself out there and expect to be successful. You got to do your work."

Bernie Williams, *outfielder, New York Yankees. San Juan, Puerto Rico. World Series Champion, 1996, 1998, 1999, 2000, 4-time Gold Glove Winner. 5-time All-star.*

"It's being able to handle yourself and know yourself as a person when you're doing great things and getting the accolades. It's also being able to be the same professional person when you're down in the dumps and things aren't going your way. The toughest thing, mentally, for me to go through was arm surgery and miss a season—going to the field every day doing all my (rehab) and knowing when the game started, I was sitting on the bench and couldn't help. I think that made me stronger as a person. It made me love the game even more. I didn't respect the fact that I had a gift that I was born with. I didn't take care of myself the way I should have and the game was taken away from me. I don't ever want to have that happen again. Therefore, I've got the respect for the game and myself that I go out and make sure that I'm in mental and physical shape to be able to play this game."

Kerry Wood, *pitcher, Chicago Cubs. Irving, Texas. NL Rookie of the Year, 1998. All-star.*

"The power of positive thought. Everything in this game is thinking, knowing, confidence and belief—all these things. It's all mental, basically. You got to do the physical things, but baseball's really taught me that day in and day out, the thoughts we think are basically what happens to us in our life. It's really made me start to scrutinize and control my thought on a daily basis."

Barry Zito, *pitcher, Oakland Athletics. Las Vegas Nevada. AL Cy Young Award Winner, 2002. 2-time All-star.*

Step up to the challenge:

- Which player's approach to being a champion did you like the best?
- How do you show up as a champion at school? At home? With your friends?
- What are some steps a champion can take to come back from a poor performance?

 ## Step out of the box to look for the signs

Try this for a week: As you go about your day, start to notice the different signs or qualities of a champion in people you know. What makes them a champion? Is it their actions, words, or attitude? How can you conduct yourself in a similar manner?

I hope you've enjoyed this book, and got to see a different side of some of your favorite baseball players and what the game has meant to them.

There's a saying, "Baseball is life." Your life isn't just a baseball season; it's all year round. Take advantage of the "home runs" these Major Leaguers have sent your way in this book. Make your experiences on the baseball field work for you off the field, too.

- Be alert and look for the signs.
- Respect your teammates and your opponents.
- Listen to your coaches.
- Play hard, play fair and above all—
- HAVE FUN!

It all starts with a step.

So keep Stepping up to the Plate!

Player Index

Player Index

About the Author

DAVID KLOSER fell in love with baseball the moment he put on his first uniform at the age of five. A former pitcher at UC Berkeley, David has been coaching baseball for over eight years in camps and high school. His FUN-damental and positive approach to the game teaches kids and young adults how to handle "curveballs" with confidence both on and off the field. David currently lives with his wife in Los Angeles.

If you'd like to receive David's FREE monthly newsletter with great sports tips, inspirational interviews, real life success strategies and more, visit www.SteppingUpToThePlate.com to sign up.

Autographs

Autographs

Autographs

Autographs

Autographs